First Topics 2

A Photocopiable Activity Book

by Pat Lamb

Introduction

First Topics 2 is a photocopiable activity book which gives a wide range of exciting activities for use with Upper Nursery, Reception and Year 1 classes. Each photocopiable sheet comes with teacher's notes which give suggestions for the further development of the activities in the classroon context. The activities can be found in themes chosen because of their suitability for this age range. These include: The Three Little Pigs, Summer, Light and Dark, Winter. It is envisaged that the busy classroom teacher will use his/her professional judgment to select activities appropriate to his/her own individual situation.

First Topics, the first book in this series, covers the themes Autumn, Teddy Bears Picnic, Gifts and Homes. Other books for "Early Years children" are also available from "Topical Resources". Please telephone for latest catalogue.

Copyright © 1996 Pat Lamb.
Illustrated by Pat Lamb.
Printed in Great Britain for "Topical Resources", Publishers of Educational Materials, P.O. Box 329, Broughton, Preston. PR3 5LT

(Tel/Fax 01772 863158)

by T.Snape & Co.Ltd., Boltons Court, Preston. Cover Design: Paul Sealey Illustration & Design, 1 Crompton House, Carr Rd, Cleveleys.

Typeset by "Topical Resources".
First Published September 1996
ISBN 1 - 872977 - 26 - X

Contents

The three little pigs

Read the story of 'The three little pigs' to the children and discuss generally.

Dot-To-Dot Pig

• Ask the children, 'Where do we see pigs? Talk about their life on the farm, appearance, cleanliness, sounds they make (squeal, grunt). What is a hog, sow, piglet! Why do they have curly tails? Draw/paint a large pig, discuss and label body parts with children.

• Children complete the pig on the sheet by joining the dots and colouring. Then, using the large pig as reference join the labels on the sheet to the body parts or, cut out labels and stick onto the pig. Cut out the pig carefully.

• Use the 'cut-out' pigs as a border around a large painted frieze of a mother pig feeding her babies and the children's writing - 'All about farm pigs'.

A Wolf Jigsaw Puzzle

• Look at pictures/books about wolves. Talk to the children about their habitat, appearance, how they live and hunt in packs etc. Point out that wolves are close relatives of dogs.

• Discuss the character of the wolf in the story. Children write over the sentence, 'Here is the bad wolf' /cut off and put in a safe place. Cut out the pieces of the puzzle, assemble correctly, stick onto a piece of paper and colour. Finish by sticking the sentence below the puzzle.

• Tell the story of 'Peter and the wolf' - Prokofiev. Listen to passages of the music. Explain the different instruments. Try to recognise when they are played again.

What Shall We Take?

• Ask the children what they think the three little pigs should take with them when they leave home. Encourage ideas about food, clothes, tools for building a house, etc. What did they use to carry their things?

• Discuss the articles on the sheet. Ask the children to choose 4 (5, 6 or 7) of them and either colour/cut around the shapes and stick onto the list or, write the names of the items on the list, adding one more that they think of.

• Children cut out pictures from catalogues to make sets of tools for building, items needed in a kitchen, bedroom, bags/suitcases for carrying items.

Which Way Shall We Go?

• Encourage the children to think carefully about things they see and hear on their route to school. Do you follow the same route? Would you see the same things if you lived in the country/a town/by the sea? What are the differences?

• Discuss what the pigs might see/pass on their journey from the farm. Complete the tracking exercise on the sheet, count the animals and colour. Draw something else they might see.

• Go for a walk around the school. Plan the route before starting. Make lists of what you see/hear/go past. Encourage the children to think about how the route changes direction/introduce 'right' and 'left' as ways of describing direction.

Looking At Number Three

• Make a 'number 3' tray by placing, for example, five shoe boxes together in a row. Have available pictures/numbers/number names and ask the children to match each box by placing the objects on each lid.
e.g.

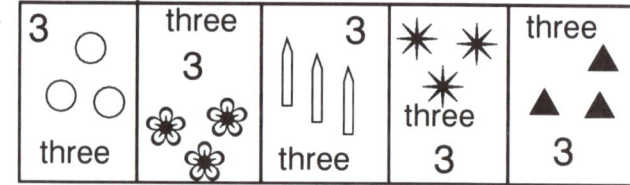

• Children complete the sheet by drawing rings to make sets of three, writing the numeral and colouring.

• Sing 'There were three furry cats', 'Count me in', A&C Black. Read 'Goldilocks and the three bears', or 'The three Billy Goats Gruff'.

Make A Mobile With Number Three

• Make sets of three by threading wooden beads, conkers, cotton reels, buttons etc.

• Children count the pigs/colour/cut out around them. Colour/cut out number three. Use a wire coathanger to make the mobile. Wrap around strips of coloured crepe paper to make it look colourful. Attach '3' to thread and hang under the hook. Attach pigs to thread and hang from the bottom of the hanger.

• Talk about triangles. Show the different kinds of triangles. Look for triangular shapes in the classroom. Put different triangles into sets/see how they tessellate.

Whose House?

• Discuss with the children the suitability of the materials-straw, sticks, bricks-chosen by the three pigs. Ask 'Which would you choose?' Give reasons for and against different materials.

• Children complete the tracking exercise to see which pig built each house/complete the sentences.

• Make collages of the three houses with suitable scrap materials. Display with the children's sentences 'the wolf blew /could not, blow this house down because......'
Sing 'The Wise man built his house upon rock', 'Okki Tokki Unga' A&C Black.

Build A House

• Choose a house near school to look at closely. Ask the children what it is made of, what materials were used for walls, windows, roof, door, chimney.

• Why were these materials chosen? Make a model house from a large box, using scrap materials and paint, and label tiles/glass/ bricks/wood.

• Discuss the parts of the house on the sheet. Children colour/cut out and assemble to make a house. Using the model as a reference label bricks, tiles, wood, glass.

• Collect/display building materials.(eg bricks, tiles, wood, sand, cement), builders tools (trowels, spade, hammer, nails etc.).
Borrow a builders helmet. Sing 'The building song' 'Alleluya'. A&C Black.

What Is Missing?
• Look at Estate Agent's brochures/book of houses, flats etc. Ask the children what features they all have in common, ie. windows, a roof. Observe different styles and colours. Think why we have a roof (to give shelter from the elements), doors (for access), windows (light and ventilation). Have all houses got chimneys? Why not?
• Discuss the houses on the sheet which all have something missing. Children draw in and label the missing part of each house. Colour.
• Paint pictures of houses/flats in bright colours. Cut out and display in a row. Sing 'I've just moved into a new house' 'Tinderbox'. A&C Black.

Brick Walls
• Examine brick walls in buildings near school. Discuss how the bricks are arranged and what holds them together. Experiment with building walls -place Lego/Duplo bricks on top of each other in rows/bond Lego/Duplo bricks. Which is the strongest?
• Children number the bricks 1-10 on the wall on top of the sheet/cut out around the wall and stick onto a piece of paper. Cut out the 10 bricks on the sheet, assemble to make a 'bonded' wall and stick onto their paper.
• Collect/paint tissue boxes. Arrange them into a 'real' wall for the home corner. How will we stick them together?

Looking At Doors
• Ask the children 'why did the wolf try to get down the chimney?'. 'Why didn't he come in through the door?' Look at the doors in the classroom. How many are there? What is there function? Are they external/internal? Discuss door furniture (hinges, handle, letterbox, keyholes, doorbells etc.). Label the different parts of the classroom door.
• Either - using placed labels on the classroom door as reference, on the sheet children draw lines from labels to the correct part of the door. Put a number on it colour and complete the sentences.
Or - colour/carefully cut the door. With the help of an adult, cut around dotted lines so that the door opens, glue onto a sheet of paper. Ask the children to pretend they are pigs/wolf. - What would the pigs see if they opened the door?/What would the wolf see if the door was opened to him? Children draw/colour a picture behind the open door. Close the door and colour the wall around the door. Write a sentence eg. 'The pigs saw the wicked wolf when they opened the door'.
• Survey the doors in school. Use unifix blocks to represent the doors and make a block graph.

The Wolf Ran Home
• Wolf begins with 'w'. Ask the children 'Can you think of other words beginning with w?' Make a list . Give the children a work sheet for sound 'w' to practice recognition and writing the letter.
• Discuss the sheet with the children. Follow the 'w' path with fingers, and then with pencil to get to the wolf's den. Colour.
• Children make up and write 'w' word sentences/draw pictures, eg. 'The wicked wolf went to the woods'. 'The wicked wolf wore white wellies'.

Story Sequence
• Ask the children to re-tell the story of 'The three little pigs', giving correct sequence of events encouraging as much detail as possible.
• Children colour/cut out the pictures and assemble in the correct order.
• In a movement lesson accompanied by percussion use instruments to dramatise the story of the three little pigs. Be 'pigs trotting happily down the lane, building a house, running from the wolf'. Be the wolf 'sneaking through the woods/huffing and puffing, running home etc'.

A Little Pig To Make
• Ask the children for ideas on how to make pigs. Give them plasticine/playdoh and let them make models of pigs. Play the 'pig game'. Each player needs a large/small ball of plasticine (body/head), four match sticks (legs), three beads (snout, eyes), two cardboard triangles (ears), a piece of pipe cleaner (tail). Throw a dice in turn. You need 6 (body) 5 (head) 4 (leg) 3 (eyes/snout) 2 (ears) 1 (tail). The winner is the first to finish the pig.
• Colour/cut out the pig on a sheet. Use paper fasteners to join the body together match 'O' and 'X'. (hang in sets of 'three' with number 3 mobiles).
• Make a 'piggy bank'. Cover a balloon with papier mache. When dry stick on four sections of an egg box for legs, one for snout, and two small thin card triangles for ears. Paint it pink with black eyes, add a pipe cleaner tail. Put a slot in the back for money.

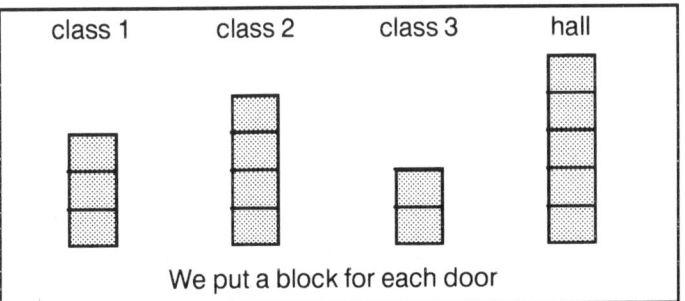

class 1	class 2	class 3	hall

We put a block for each door

Dot-to-dot pig.

ear

snout

trotter

curly tail

A wolf jigsaw puzzle.

Here is the bad wolf

What shall we take?

This is our list.

knapsack

apple

spade

nails

hammer

cup

saw

shirt

boots

Which way shall we go?

wolf

sheep

ducks

Looking at number 3.
Draw rings to make sets of 3.

red houses

pink pigs

grey wolves

Make a mobile with number 3.

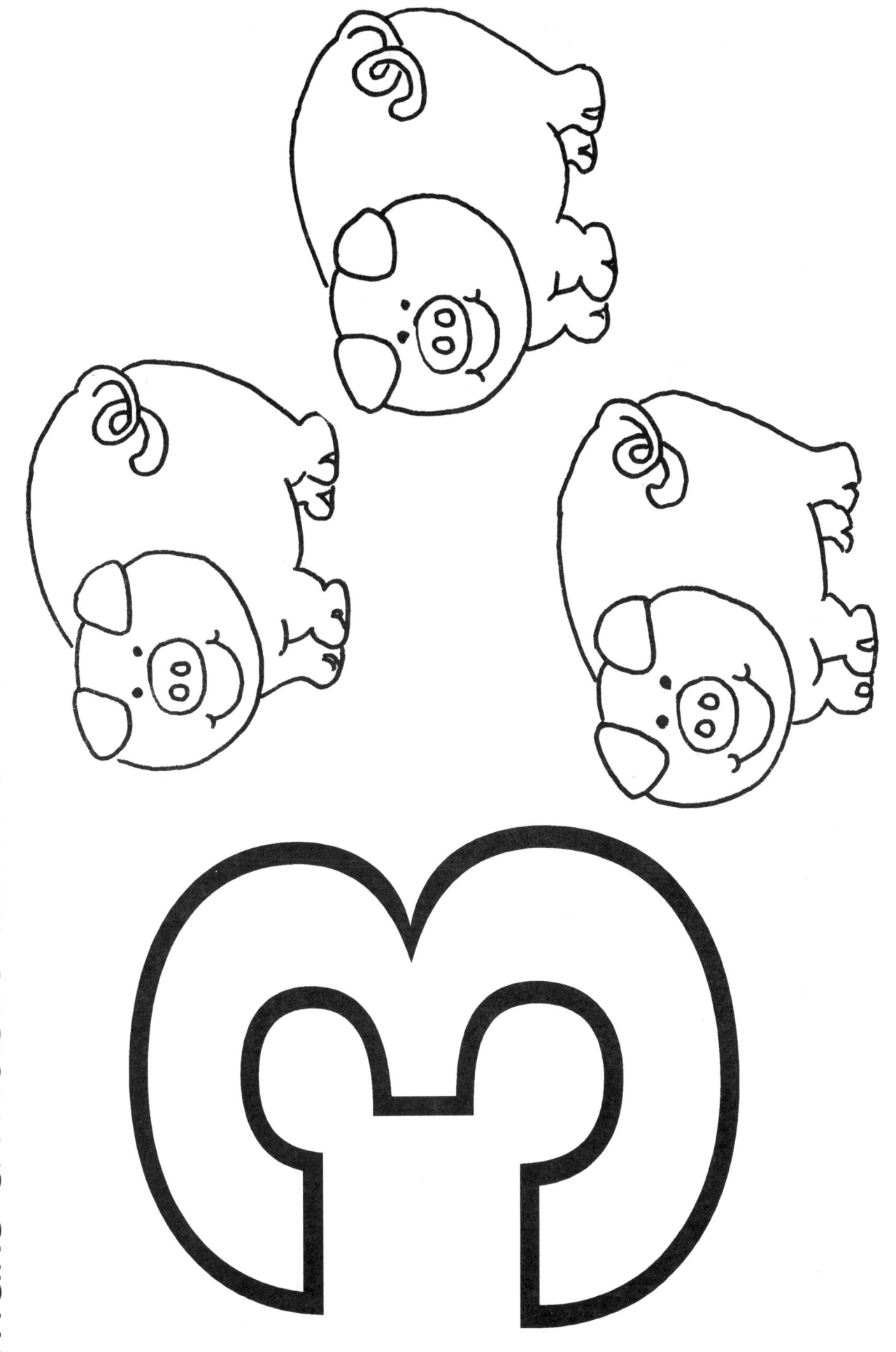

Whose house?

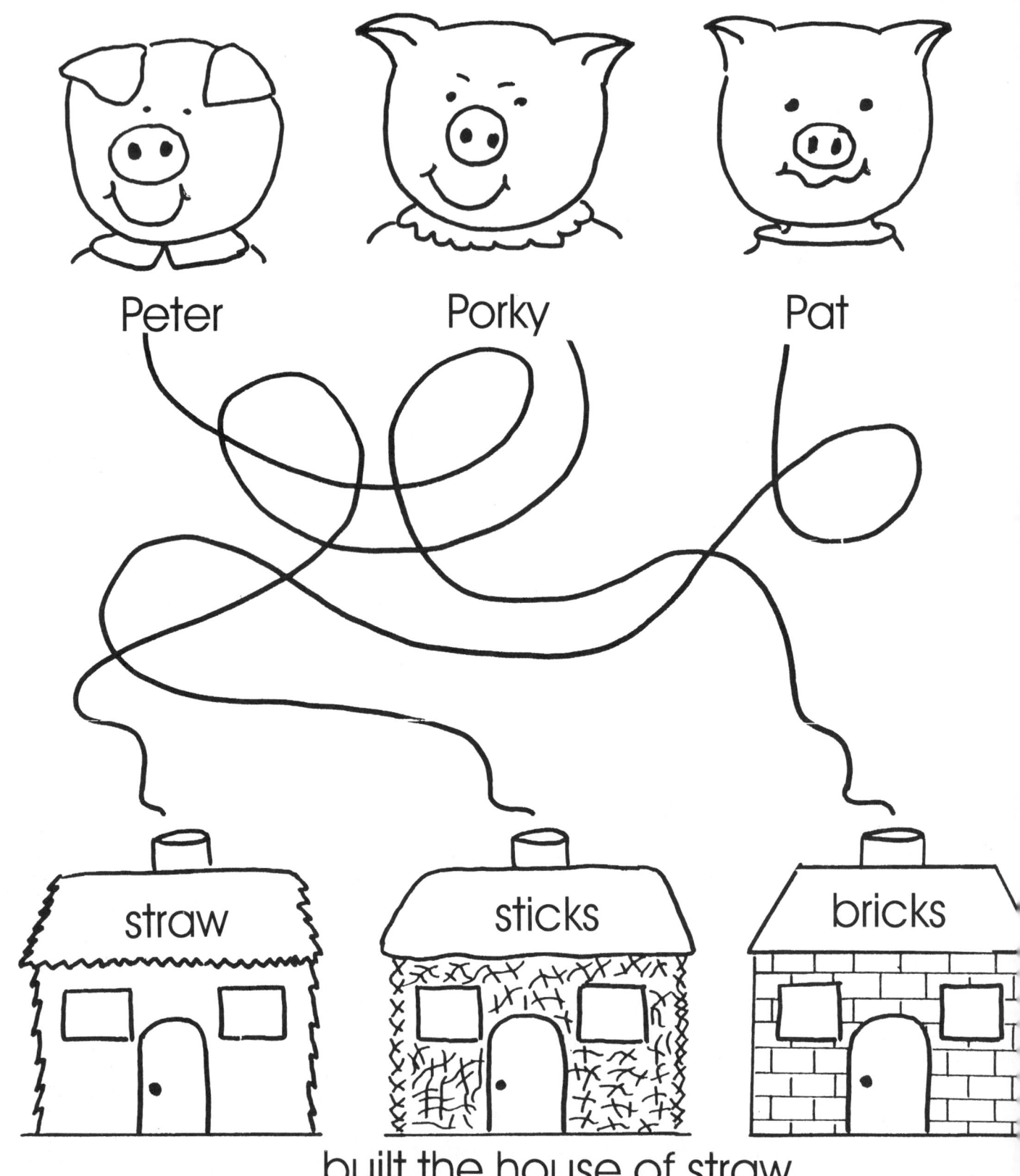

Peter

Porky

Pat

straw

sticks

bricks

_____ built the house of straw.

_____ built the house of sticks.

_____ built the house of bricks.

Build a house. What do we need?

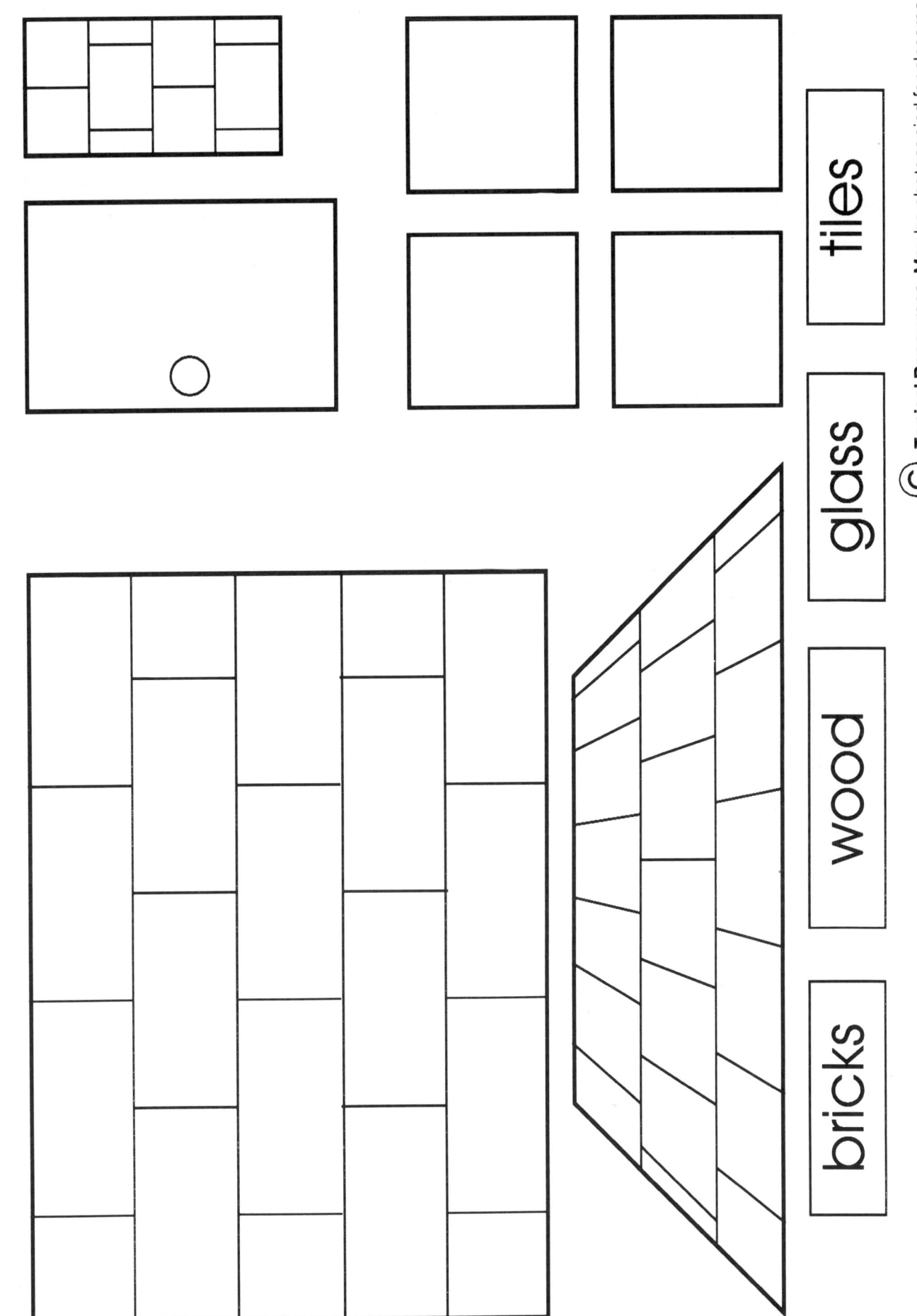

bricks   wood   glass   tiles

What is missing? Can you finish the houses?

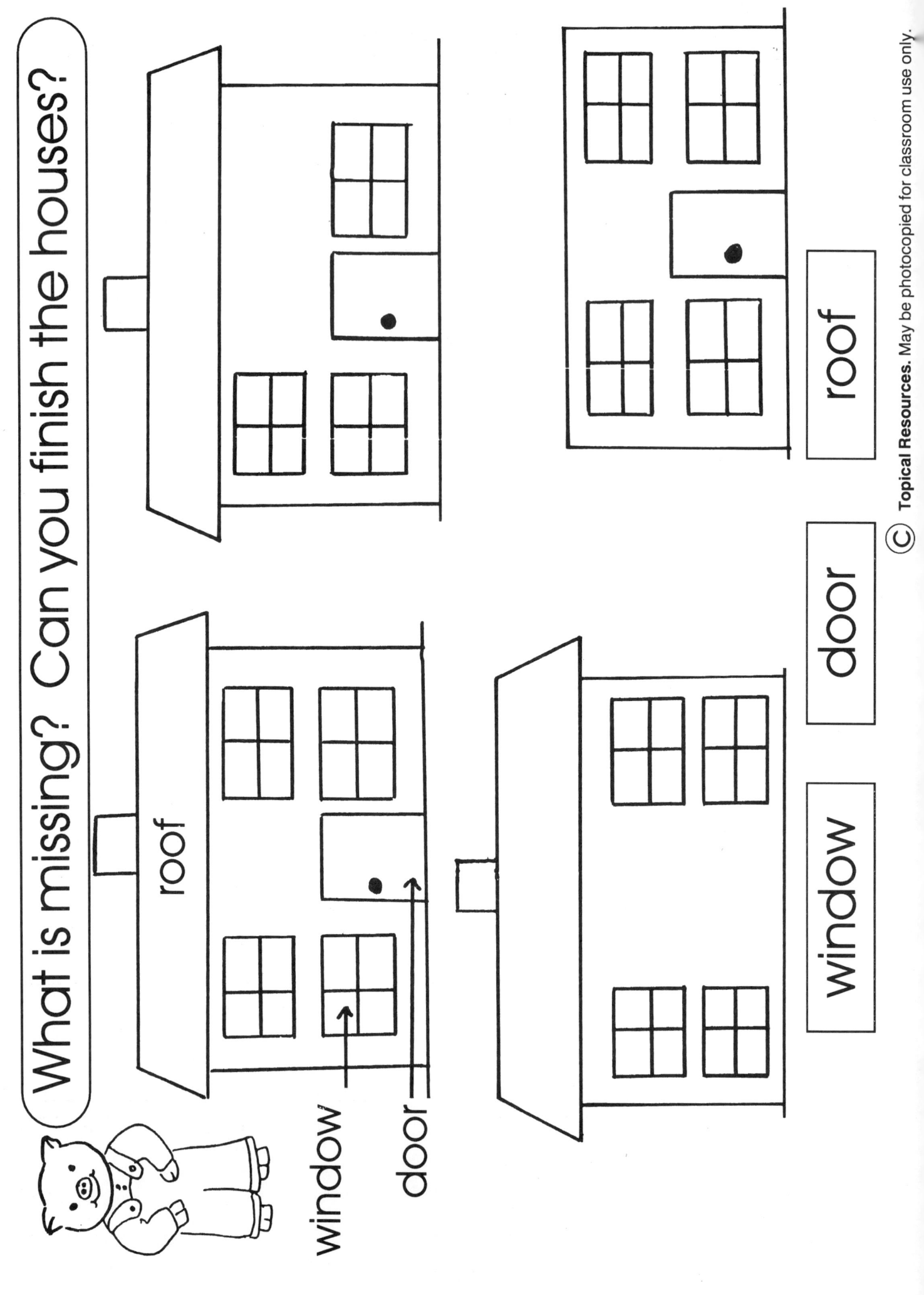

roof

door

roof

window

door

window

Brick walls.
Number the bricks.

Use these bricks to build a wall.

Looking at doors.

The wolf can't get in!

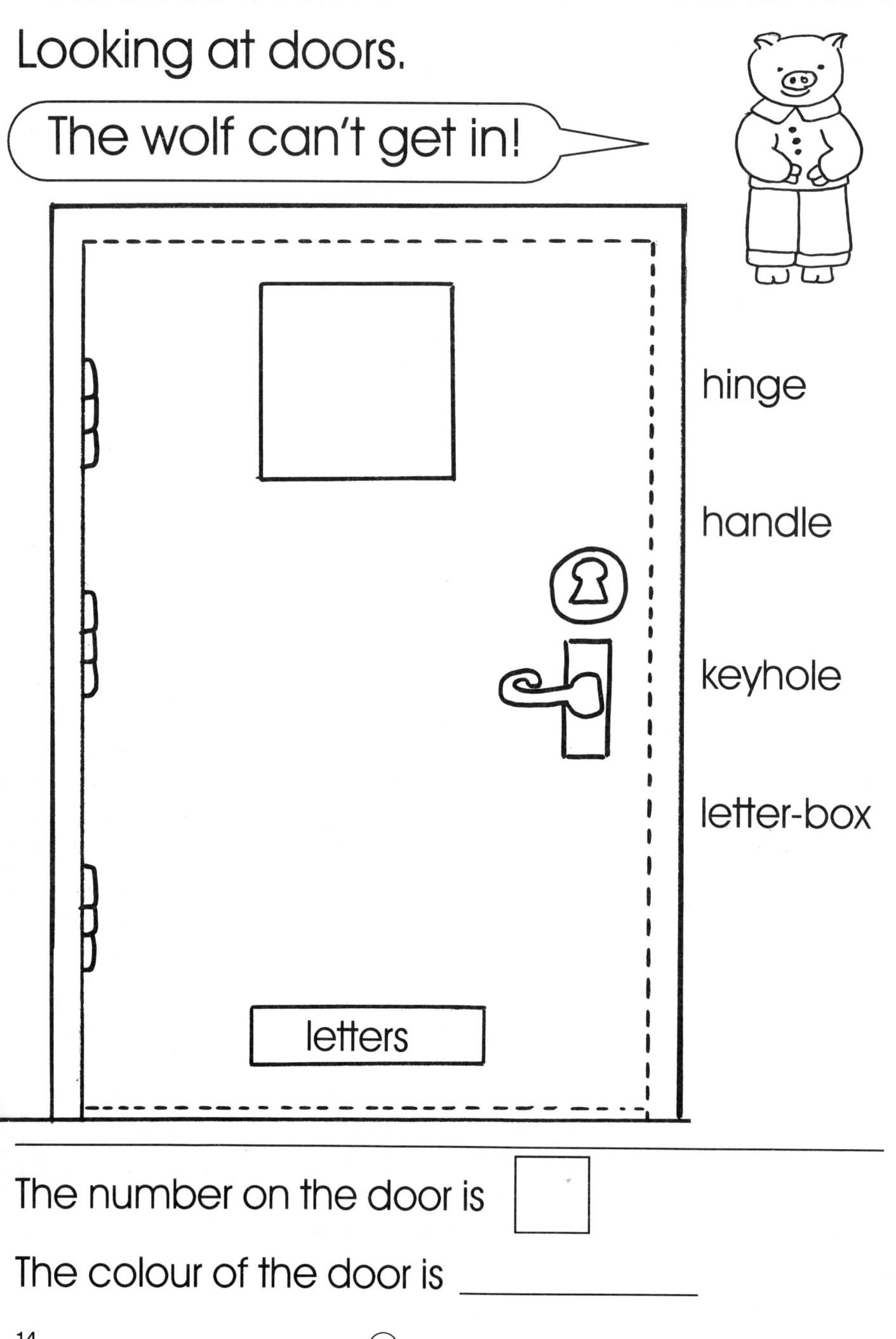

hinge

handle

keyhole

letter-box

letters

The number on the door is ☐

The colour of the door is _____

The wolf ran home.

Follow the 'w' path to get to the wolf's den.

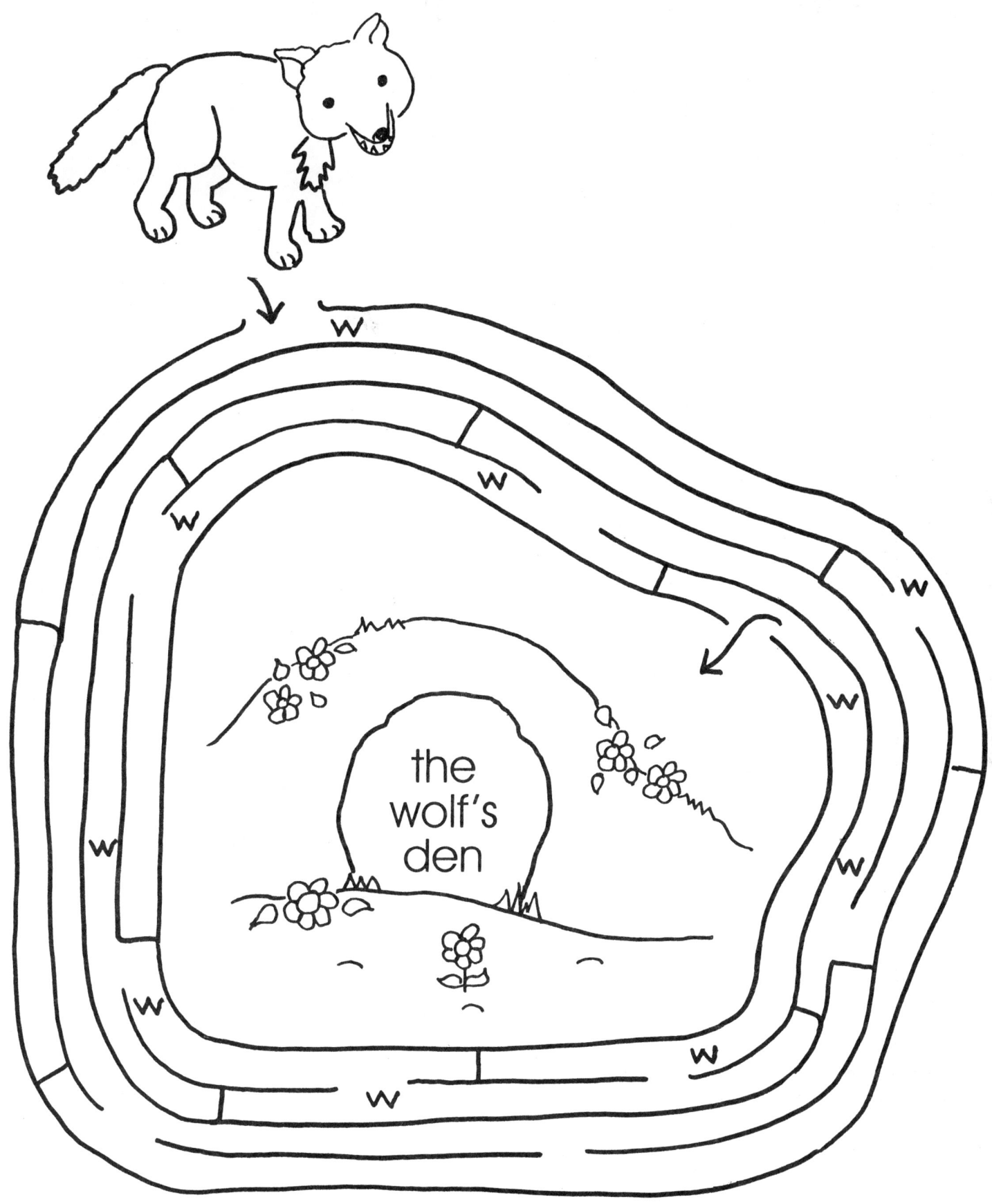

the
wolf's
den

15

Story sequence. Can you put the pictures in order?

The 3 pigs lived happily together.

The wolf could not blow down the brick house.

The wolf blew down the stick house.

The wolf blew down the straw house.

16

A little pig to make.

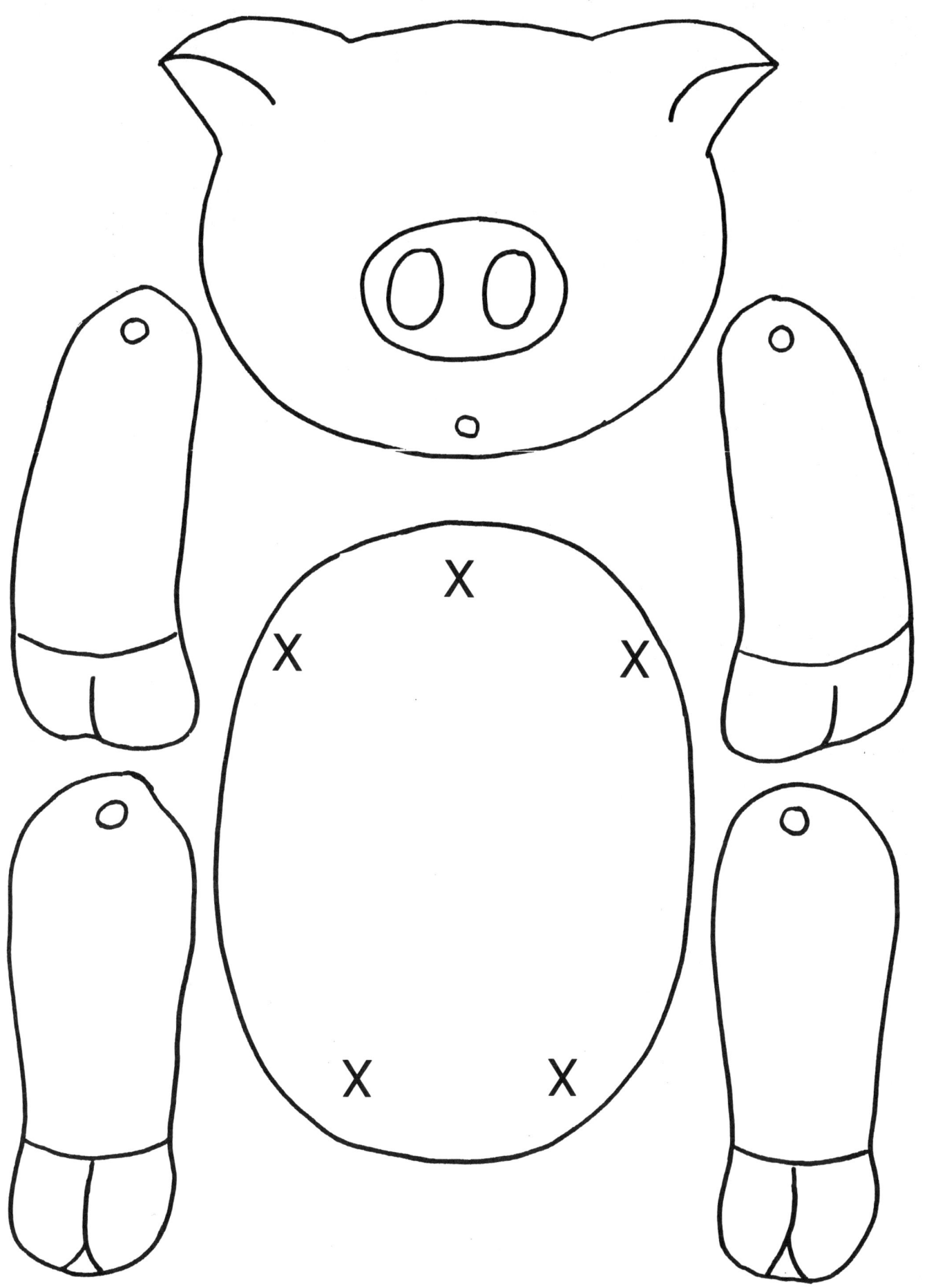

Summer

Hot Sunny Days

• Ask the children 'What do you like to do on a hot sunny day?' Choose five activities eg. picnic, swim at seaside, eat ice-cream, barbeque, play out, and make a block graph of 'Things we like to do in the sun'. Read 'Squirting Rainbows', 'Seaside' Shirley Hughes, Walker books.

• Children colour pictures/cut out around them. Stick onto a piece of paper with sentences - 'I like to have a picnic', 'Joe and Amy are wearing sun-hats' etc.

• Make a mosaic of the sun using gold foil, orange and yellow paper. Make a list of words describing hot sunny days eg. sizzling, scorching, bright, burning, etc. mount on gold/yellow paper and arrange as rays radiating from the sun. Talk about the dangers of too much sun.

A Sunny Day Puzzle

• Make a collection/ display of summer clothes - shorts, t-shirts, swimwear, sun-hats, flip-flops, sun-glasses, etc. Talk about ways of keeping cool in hot weather - wearing cool clothes, eating refreshing fruit and ice-cream, having cold drinks, paddling, sitting in the shade.

• Children cut out the labels at the bottom of the page and keep in a safe place. Cut out the pieces of the puzzle, assemble correctly, stick onto a piece of paper and colour. Finish by labelling the puzzle.

• Make ice lollies.

In The Garden

• Sing 'English country garden', 'Harlequin', A&C Black. Discuss with the children the things they would see/hear in the garden/park. (-different flowers, summer fruits, creatures such as bees, birds, butterflies, other insects etc).

• Children complete the sheet by counting and labelling the things in the garden. Colour and add a bird.

• Make 'a garden in a pot'. Plant 3 or 4 brightly coloured flowers in a large pot. Keep well watered and watch to see which creatures visit the flowers. Read ' Whose garden' M Krantz, Hawey House Publications.

Busy Bees

• Take some honey into the classroom and let the children taste it. Ask where they think it comes from. Explain how bees collect nectar from flowers and take back to the hive where honey is produced in honeycombs. Look at hexagon shapes (like honeycombs), cut some out to see how they tessellate. Use the hexagon shapes for children's writing about bees and put together to make a 'honeycomb'.

• Children complete the writing patterns on the page and colour.

• Make bees from cardboard rolls painted with black and yellow stripes. Use white tissue for head and wings. Read 'Harry's bee' P. Campbell, Puffin. Make up prayers to say thank you for this gift of food.

Can You Match The Butterflies

• Read 'The very hungry caterpillar' Eric Carle. Sing 'I went to see the cabbages', 'Tinderbox', A&C Black. Talk about the life cycle of the butterfly. Look at books of different kinds of butterflies. Can you identify any?

• Children match the butterflies on the sheet by drawing lines and colouring each pair the same.

• Make 'fold-over' butterflies. Dab blobs of different coloured paint on to one half of a piece of paper. Fold the paper and press down firmly. Open and reveal a 'beautiful butterfly'. Cut out and decorate with sequins, glitter and beads.

Ladybirds

• Sing 'Ladybird', 'Tinderbox', A&C Black. Look at pictures/books of ladybirds. Talk about their appearance, when we see them, use in gardens and what they feel like when they run across your hand.

• Children count the spots on each ladybird and match to a number. Colour.

• Make a felt ladybird. You need 2 oval body shapes (black and red), a black felt head shape, 6 pieces of pipecleaner, black buttons, black and white felt scraps.

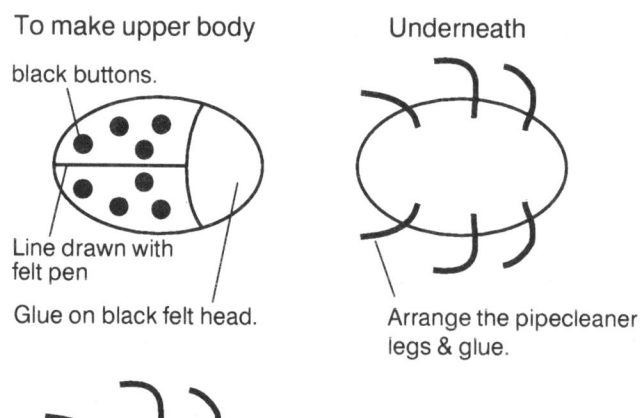

To make upper body

black buttons.

Line drawn with felt pen

Glue on black felt head.

Underneath

Arrange the pipecleaner legs & glue.

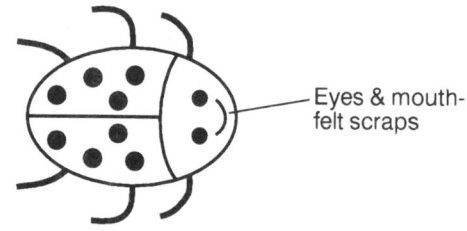

Eyes & mouth- felt scraps

Glue the 2 body parts together leaving a gap at the bottom. Stuff with tissue & join gap.

Make A Flower
• Sing 'Think of a world without any flowers' Someone's singing Lord, A&C Black. Bring flowers into school from the garden /countryside. Consider colours, shape, smell. Make comparisons. Collect and display seed packets. Paint pictures for 'a flower exhibition'.
• Colour brightly and cut out the flower parts. Pleat the rectangle following the dotted lines. Find the centre of the pleated paper and secure with a paperclip/staple. Fan the ends out and glue together to make a circle. Glue the centre circle in place. Paint an art straw green and attach leaves and flower. Make into a 'number line garden'.
• Talk about different part of the flower. Draw/label roots, stem, petals, leaves.

Summer Food
• Talk about the food we enjoy in the summer - salads, fruit, ice-cream, yoghurts. Make lists of fruit grown here/other countries. Ask the children to bring some fruit to put in the fruit bowl to share.
• Children colour the fruit in the bowl and on the labels. Cut out labels. Complete the tracking exercise and glue the labels in the correct place.
• Make a pictogram of favourite fruits. Make fresh fruit juice and drink it at play time.

Going On Holiday
• Discuss with the children what they would need for a holiday by the sea. Make a list with pictures. (don't forget rainy day clothes). 'What will you carry the things in?'
• Finish the suitcase on the sheet by joining the dots, colour, cut out. Choose 5 (6/7) things that you would like to take on holiday, colour, cut around them and glue in suitcase, or write a list of the chosen articles.
• Make a suitcase out of a box with a lid. Cover with material or paint. Use a catalogue to choose a holiday wardrobe for yourself, mum, dad, gran, etc. Cut around the things you have chosen and 'pack' in your case.

Travelling To The Seaside
• Read 'Topsy and Tim go on a train'. Ask the children to think about a long journey they have made. How did they get there? Make a collection/display of toy cars, trains, aeroplanes, boats, etc.
• Use the sheet as (a) number exercise. Draw 2 people in the car, 3 in the coach, 4 in the train, 5 in the plane. Or (b) make a survey of how children travelled when they went on holiday. eg. draw 2 people in the coach, colour, cut out and write a sentence 'Joe and Suzy went on a coach', etc.
• Arrange a class trip by coach to a railway station, travel a few miles by train and arrange to be picked up at your new destination - so the children can experience and compare the two modes of travel.

Where Shall We Stay
• Turn the creative play area into a 'caravan'. Make sleeping, cooking, eating areas etc. Discuss a caravan site with the children. What is on the site? - shop, toilets, play area, cafe.
• Children complete the caravan on the sheet by joining the numbers 1-10, labelling and colouring. Use the cut-out caravans to make a 'caravan site' adding shop, cafe etc.
• Have available various brochures/magazines showing different sorts of holidays for children to look at. Discuss the different places they have stayed - hotel, tent, caravan, boat, farm house, and make into a block graph. Which was most popular?

On The Beach
• Sing 'Oh I do like to be beside the seaside'. Talk to the children about all the different things they may see on the beach/different activities they can do - swim, look for shells, picnic, watch seagulls etc. Draw pictures/write sentences.
• Discuss objects/activities on the sheet. 'Seaside' begins with 's'. Can you see anything that begins with 's'? Cut out the labels and glue onto the correct object on the picture. Find other 's' words and circle or label. Draw a seagull and colour.
• Ask the children to bring photographs of themselves, mum and dad, grans and grandads at the seaside. Display and make comparisons.
Read 'Postman Pat at the seaside'.

Sports Day
• In a P.E. lesson have lots of fun races outside in the sunshine, - running, skipping, with balls, hoops, beanbags. Encourage the children to help in organising the races eg. 'Amy can you put ten children in this race?' 'Joe give them all a red beanbag'.
• Children count, number and colour the sacks on the sheet.
• Arrange a class 'sports day'. Devise a race for mums and dads. Make rosettes for everyone who takes part.

A Walk In The Park
• Go for a walk in the park. Look at the trees, flowers, sky. Run on the grass (if allowed). Listen to the sounds. Smell flowers, fresh cut grass. 'What can we do there?' - feed the ducks, play games, go on the swings etc. 'Can you spot any bees, butterflies, other insects?' Have a picnic.
• Discuss the items on the sheet. See how many the children observed on their walk and colour these in.
• Children draw/paint a picture of themselves. Cut these out and attach to the children's writing, in a speech bubble, of something they saw/heard in the park. Display around a collage of the duckpond or adventure playground.

Hot sunny days. What shall we do?

A sunny day puzzle. Keeping cool.

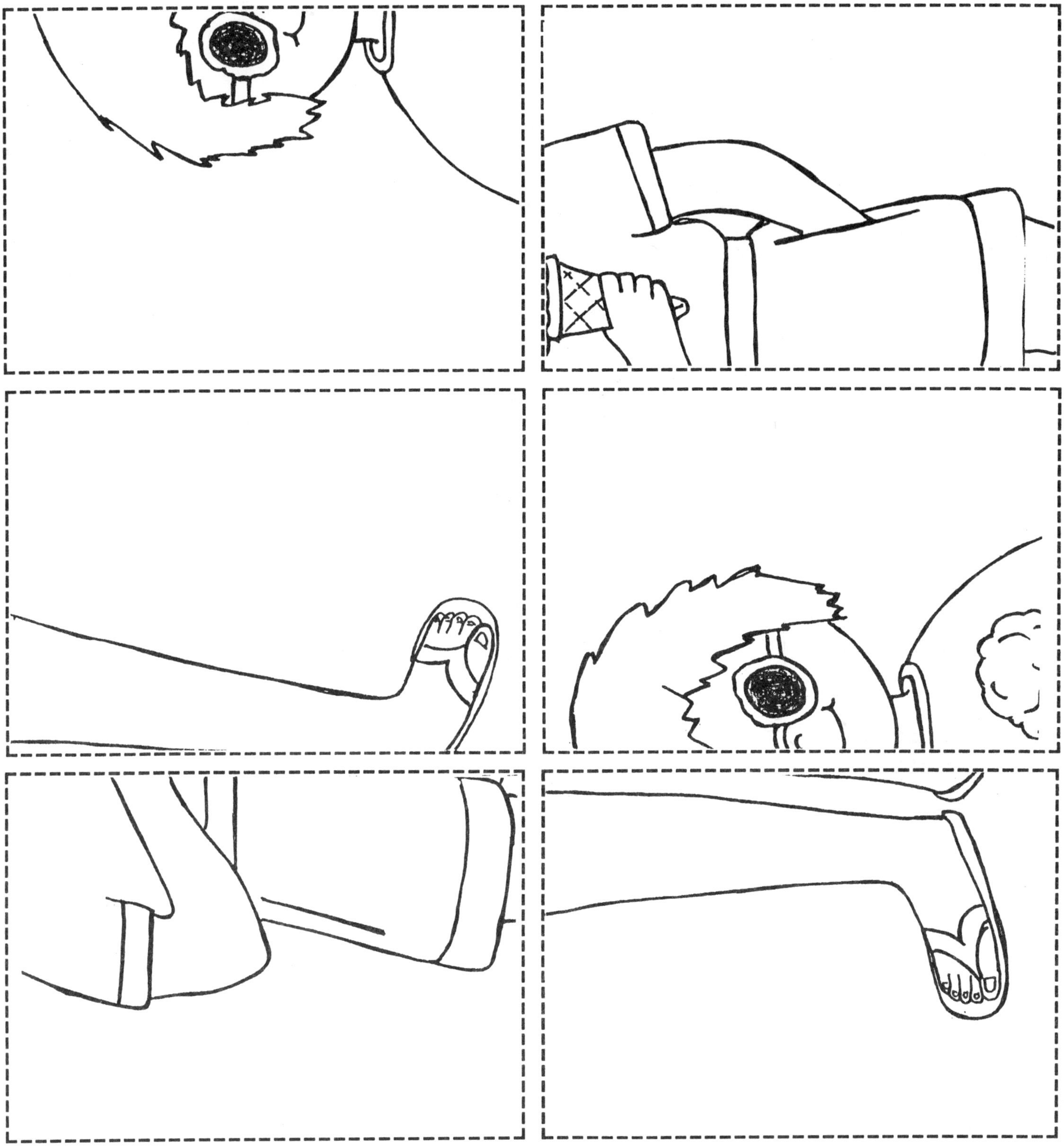

| ice-cream  | sun-glasses  |
| flip-flops 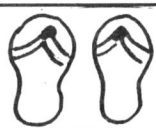 | shorts  |

In the garden. How many?

worms

strawberries

bees

butterflies

flowers

22

Busy Bees.

buzz....zzzz

buzz....zzzz

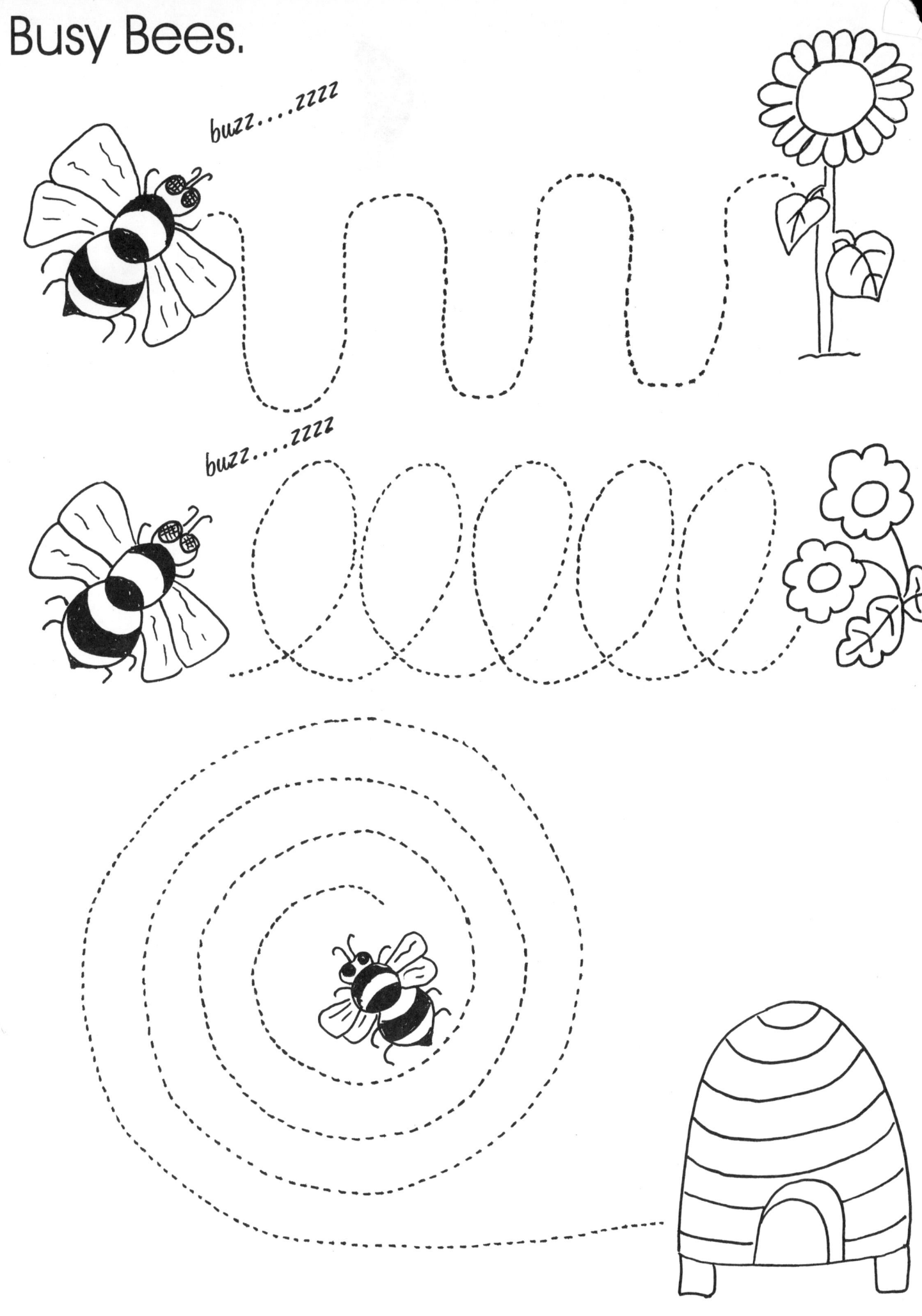

23

Can you match the butterflies?

Ladybirds.

How many spots on each ladybird?

1

2

3

4

5

Make a flower.

centre

leaf

fold

26

Summer food. The fruit bowl.

strawberry

apple

orange

grapes

Going on holiday.

towel

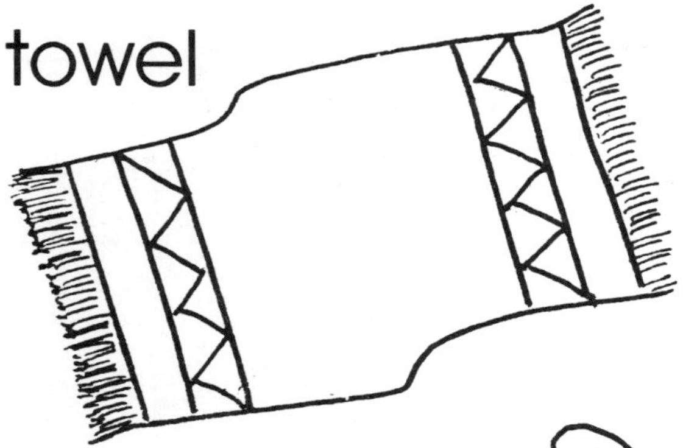

bucket and spade

ball

teddy bear

hat

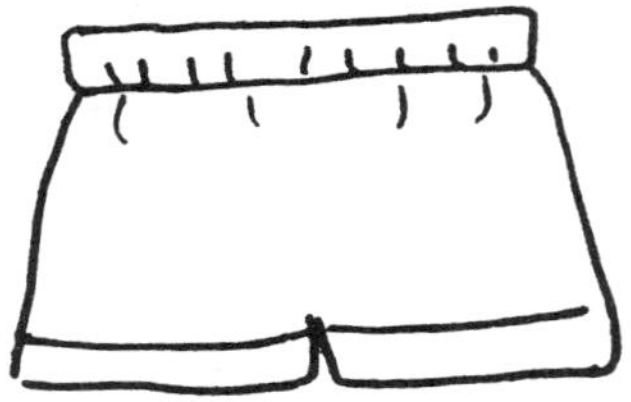

shorts

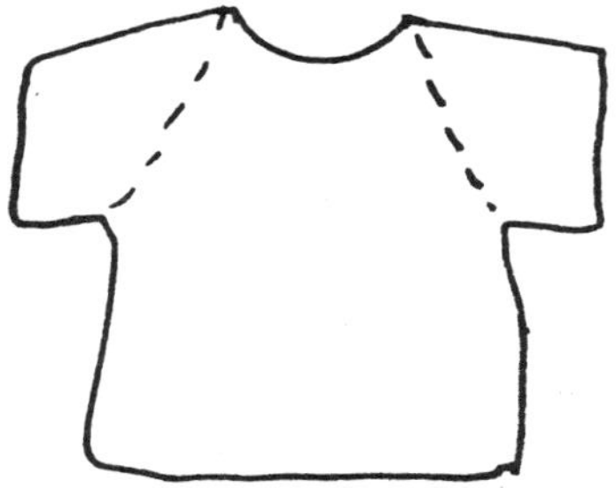

T-shirt

sun-glasses

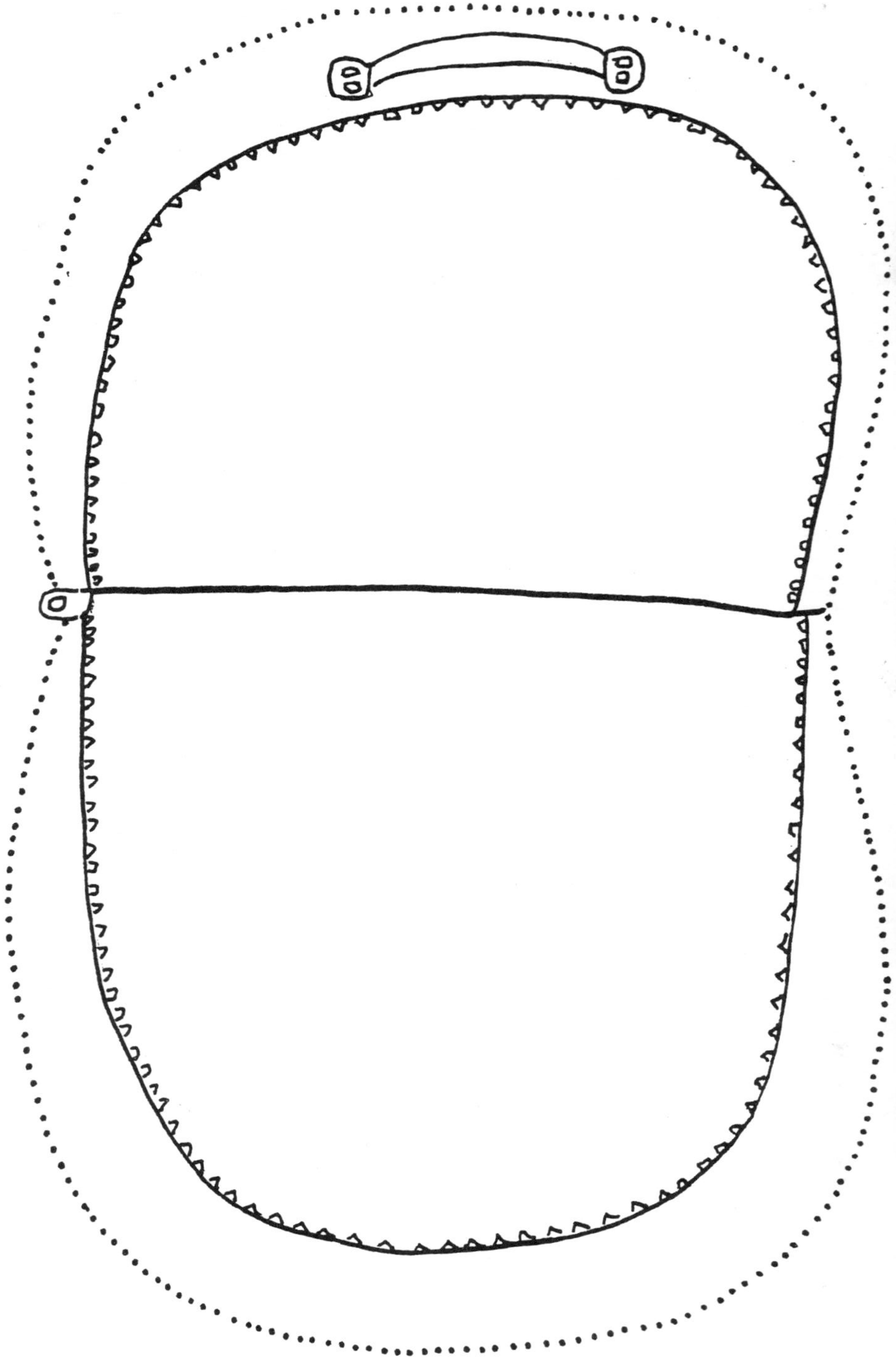

Travelling to the seaside. How shall we get there?

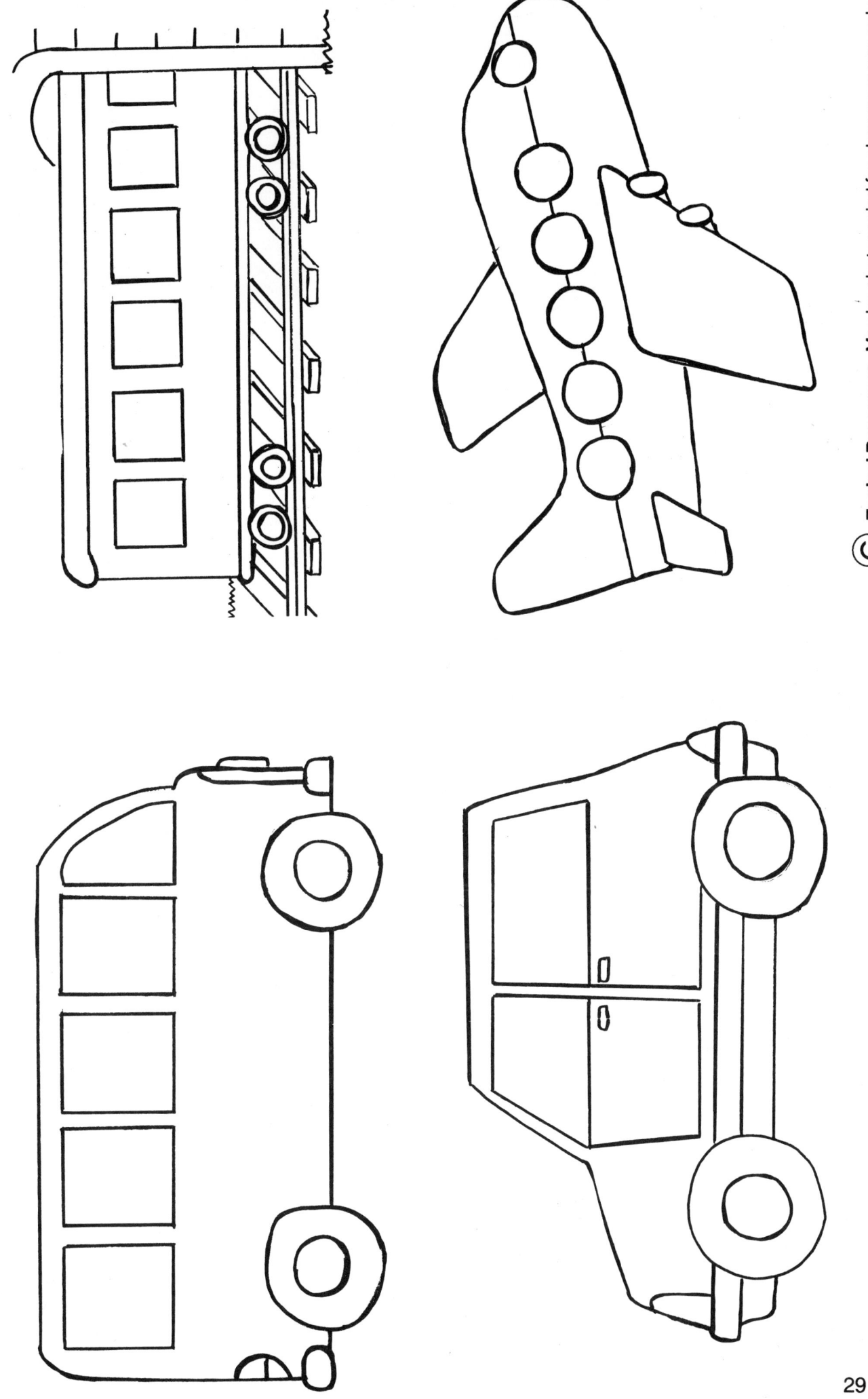

29

Where shall we stay? Join the numbers to finish the caravan.

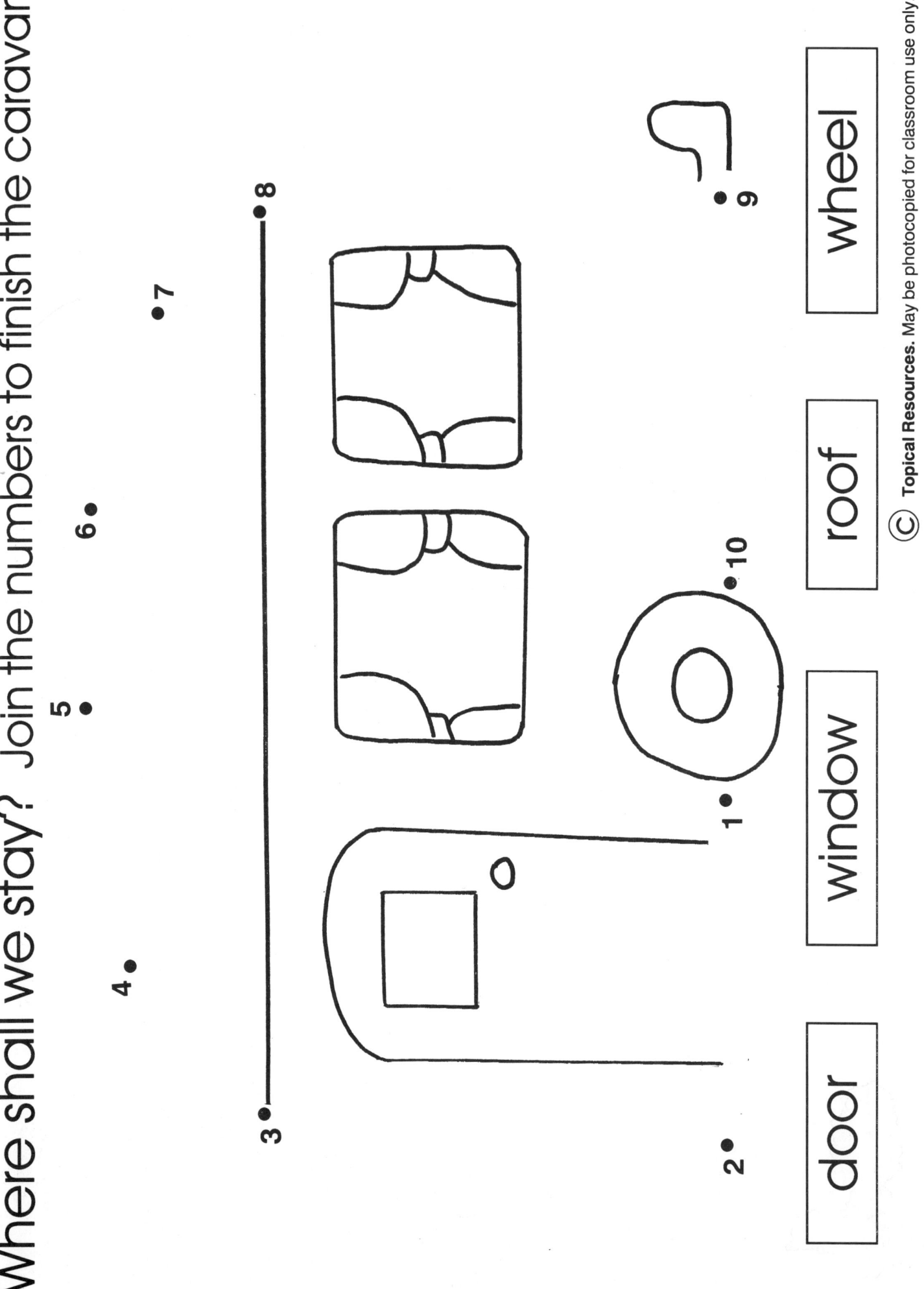

door   window   roof   wheel

On the beach.

spade | starfish | sea | sandcastle | sun

31

Sports day. The sack race.

Count the sacks. Number the sacks.

Colour the sacks.

Number 1 is red.
Number 2 is blue.
Number 3 is yellow.
Number 4 is green.
Number 5 is brown.

32

A walk in the park. Did you see...?

33

The Moon

• Sing 'Hey diddle diddle'.
Look at a night time picture. What can we see in the sky? What is the moon? Explain why it shines at night/what causes it to change shape. What is moonlight/ a moonbeam? Talk about the American moon landings/show a video of them.

• Use the sheet to record the childrens' writing about the moon. Children complete numbers 1-5 on rocket/colour. The childrens' writing can be cut out, mounted on silver paper, and made into mobiles.

• Make a moon picture. Cut a large circle of white paper and glue onto dark blue. Give the children a template of an owl/bat to draw round on black paper/cut out. Glue onto picture, overlapping the moon and into the sky. Add silver stars.

Twinkle, Twinkle, Little Star

• Sing 'Twinkle, twinkle, little star'. When do we see stars? What does the sky look like on a starry night? Make a collection of words that describe stars (twinkle/ glitter/ sparkle/ shine).

• Use the sheet as a number and writing activity. Join the dots 1-10 to make a star, and join the dots to finish the other stars. Label 'a big star' and 'a little star'. Colour yellow/add glitter to make them 'twinkle'.

• Make six-pointed stars with art straws.

The Sun

• Sing 'The sun has got his hat on'. Talk about the shape/colour of the sun. Explain that it is a very large star, nearer to the earth than other stars, that it provides us with warmth and light, and how even on very cloudy days the sun's beams of light are strong enough to give us daylight. Ask the children what they think would happen if it suddenly stopped shining.

• Children join the dots to complete the sun's face/colour/cut out (younger children will need help with cutting). Cut out the hat, colour, and decorate with sequins, beads, ribbon, feathers - and stick onto the sun.

• Explain how all living things - animals, birds, insects, people, need light and warmth from the sun. With the children, plant some seeds in pots. Place some in direct sunlight, some in the shade, and some in a dark cupboard. Let the children observe the effects of too much or too little light and warmth.

• WARNING - It is dangerous to look directly at the sun.

A Night Or Day Picture

• Explain simply why we have night and day. Read 'day and night' by David Bennett. 'Bear Facts'. Mulberry. Talk about/ make lists of the differences between day and night, and day-time and night-time activities.

• Look at the picture and discuss. Divide the class. Ask some of the children to make a 'day-time' picture - colour the sky blue, add clouds and the sun, dad is cleaning the car, children playing, cows in the field etc. Ask other children to make a 'night-time' picture - moon/stars in dark

sky, car headlights on, someone working with a torch, owl in tree etc. Make comparisons.

• Make a street frieze by day/night. Some children paint houses in bright colours/cut out and put onto a background with blue sky, sun, clouds, etc. Others cut out silhouette houses, with gold foil for lighted windows, and glued onto a dark blue/black sponge printed sky, with moon and stars in silver foil.

Sunshine And Shadows

• On a sunny day go into the playground with the children. Look at the shadows. Run away from your shadow, play shadow games (statues, tag). Look at your shadow when you jump. Go into a shady place - can you see your shadow now? Why not? Are shadows in front or behind you? Help them realise that the sun is on one side, shadow on other.

• Children look at their/each other's shadows when they do the actions on the sheet - stand, hop, stretch, kick with ball. Complete the sheet by matching the body shape with the shadow and labelling.

• Children discuss things they can do /shadows can't (eg. talk, eat, read) and vice versa (eg. change shape, disappear) and write sentences, with a drawing of themselves and their shadow.

Or. Make a 'shadow' clock to see how the sun moves throughout the day. Place a bottle on a piece of paper in the sunshine/draw around the shadow after assembly, morning play etc. Note the different shape/positions of the shadows.

Times Of The Day

• Discuss the sequence of morning, afternoon, evening etc., and daily routines - getting up, breakfast, coming to school etc. Talk about the pattern of the school day - assembly, lunch, play times, hometime etc. Paint pictures/write sentences of 'our day at school' and arrange in sequence along the wall.

• Children cut out the sentences and place on the correct picture. Colour the picture/cut out/arrange. Glue in the correct order onto a piece of paper.

• Ask the children 'How do we know when it is time for play?' Talk about clocks/look at pictures of famous clocks (Big Ben etc.). Make a collection of clocks and watches and listen to their sounds - alarms, ticks, chimes. Sing 'Hickory dickory dock', sing 'At 1/2 past three we go home to tea', 'Someone's singing Lord', A&C Black.

Dress Teddy For Bed

•Talk about the need for sleep. How do we feel when we become tired - we are bad-tempered, make mistakes, forget things etc. Make a collection/display of nightwear - nightie, pyjamas, slippers, teddy, dressing gown, hot water bottle.

•(These pictures may need to be enlarged). Talk about the clothes on the sheet. Children colour/cut out the bear and clothes of their choice. 'Dress' the bear by sticking clothes onto it with blu-tac.

•Design a bed for teddy, using cardboard boxes and scrap materials OR Make sets of slippers, beds, nighties etc. cut from magazines.

There Were 10 In A Bed

•Discuss bedtime routines - bathtime, supper, mum/dad reading a story, snuggling in bed with a favourite toy. Children draw pictures/write sentences about 'bedtime'.

•Learn/sing the song 'There were 10 in the bed'. Use the sheet as a number activity. Count the children in bed, write the numbers 1-10 above each child's head. Choose/write a name for each child.

•Act out the song. Put 10 chairs in a row, with a child on each chair. Sing the song and as each verse is finished one child leaves a chair, until only one is left. As each child leaves ask 'how many are left now?' 'How many would be left if two fell out?' etc.

Creatures Out And About by Day And Night

•Choose some nocturnal creatures eg. badger, fox, bat, owl. Look at books/pictures. Think about what makes them different to those that come out in the daytime - appearance, habitat, activities etc. Paint/draw pictures, write simple sentences about the animals.

•Discuss the creatures on the sheet, colour, cut out around each one. Provide the children with two large paper circles. Arrange so they overlap and glue together. Sort the creatures into sets of those out at night/during the day/ seen by day or night. Add other creatures to the set.

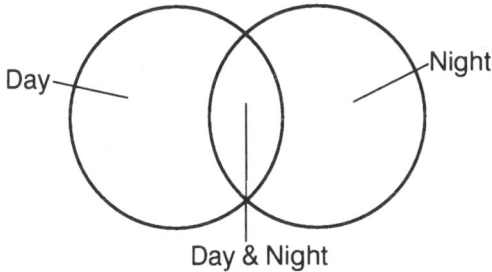

•Invite a policeman/nurse/fireman into school to talk about their work, and how they are there to help us both during the day and by night.

Make An Owl

•Read 'Goodnight owl' by P. Hutchinson. Puffin. Look at pictures/books about owls. The owl is nocturnal. What does this mean? Discuss the owl's appearance, habitat, the sound it makes, how it hunts, and what it eats. What is an 'owl pellet?' What do the contents tell us?

•Using owl pictures as reference, children colour in the body parts of the owl. Cut out and assemble. Have available some strips of fringed brown crepe paper for the children to stick onto the wings to give a 3D effect.

•Use the owls to make a number line. Cut up an old pair of tights, stretch and pin onto a branch shape on a dark background. Place the owls in a line on the branch and number 1-10.

Underground Tunnel

•Investigate animals that live underground - mole, badger, rabbits etc. What are their homes called? Where/how do they make them? Why do you think they choose to live underground? Keep worms for a short time so that the children can observe the way they live, move, under the soil.

•Ask the children 'How do you know where a mole has been?' Explain about mole hills and how they are made. Children can complete the tracking exercise on the sheet.

•Who has been through a tunnel in a train or car? Why were tunnels built? Has anyone been through the Channel Tunnel? What is special about it? Collect pictures and display. Make tunnels in the sand tray for your cars to go through.

Looking At Lights

•Talk about when/why we need lights. Have available candle, torch, electric lamp. Discuss/ demonstrate how each gives us light. What provides the power for torch/lamp? Make lists/draw pictures of where we see light from candles, batteries, electricity. Where do traffic and street lights get their power from?

•Discuss all the objects on the sheet. Children circle/colour the odd one out.

•Experiment with batteries and make a simple circuit to light a bulb. Talk about how we can see at night. Find examples of reflective and luminous clothing for road safety.

Different Candles

•Make a collection of candles and display. Sort them according to colour, shape, size. Are some scented/decorated? Talk about what they are made of, feel like. Light a candle (talk about safety) watch the flame, smell it burning. Does it give much light? Why were they important in the past?

•Make and study a set of thin/thick candles and label. Discuss the candles on the sheet and label thick/thin. Count/write the numbers of candles in each set/complete the sentence/colour.

•Candles are important in religious festivals such as Diwali, Chanukah, at a Christmas service, Sweden's Festival of Light, where they represent comfort, light, love etc. Explore one of these festivals and make and light candles, a 'Christingle' etc.

The moon

Twinkle, twinkle little star.
Join the dots to finish the stars.

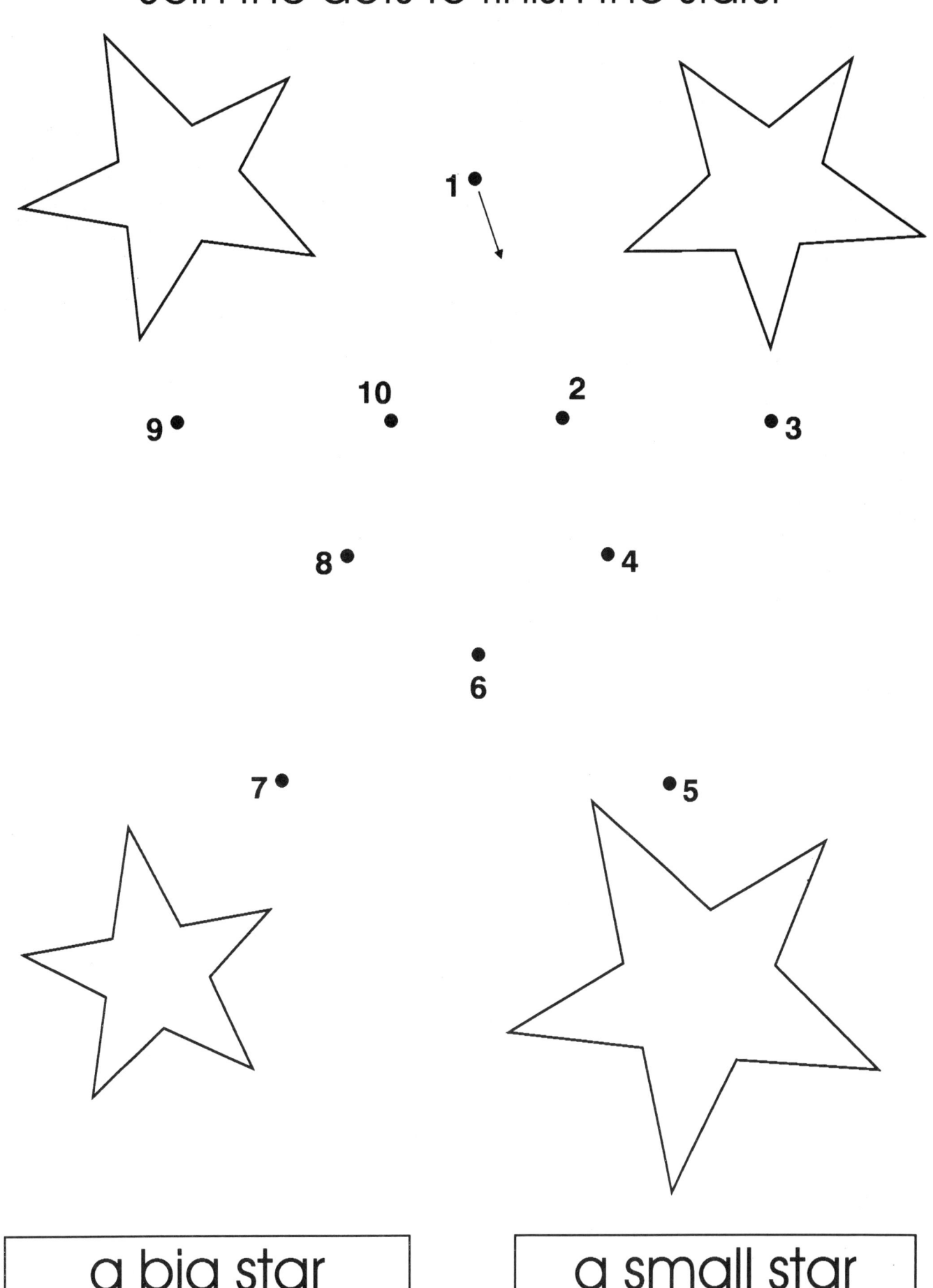

a big star

a small star

37

The sun.

A night or day picture to colour.

39

Sunshine and shadows. Help Jack to find his shadow.

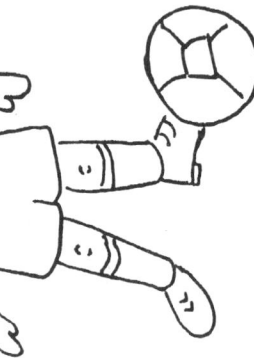

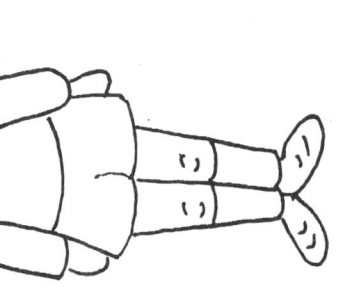

standing

kicking

hopping

stretching

Times of the day.

Time to get up.

Time for school.

Time for dinner.

Time to relax.

Dress the teddy bear for bed.

There were 10 in a bed. Put a number above each child.

Give each child a name.

Jack

43

Creatures -
out and about by day or night

mouse

rabbit

butterfly

cat

fox

bee

hen

squirrel

owl

hedgehog

bat

Make an owl.

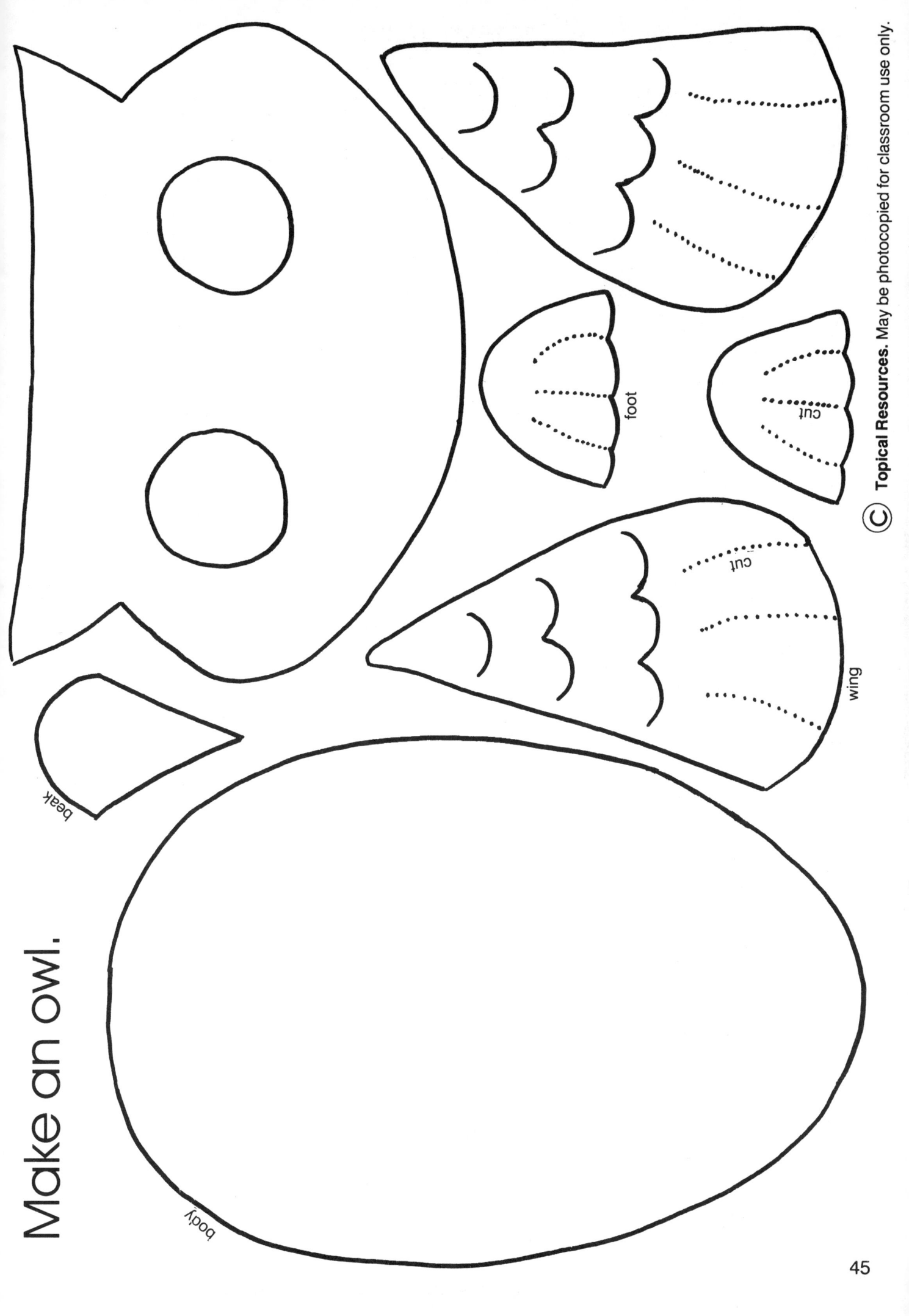

foot

cut

wing

cut

beak

body

Underground tunnels.

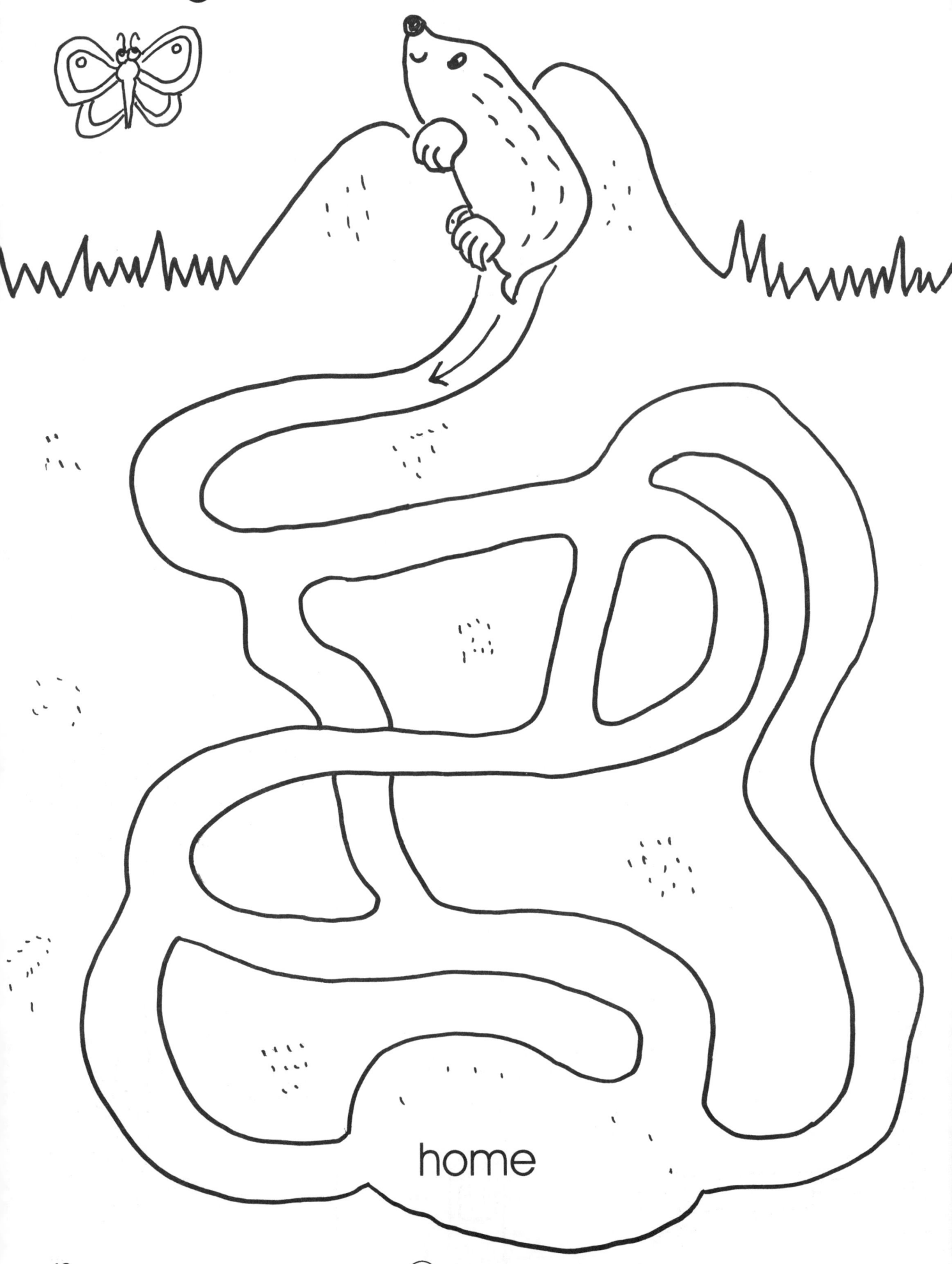

home

Looking at lights. Which one is different?

47

Different candles.

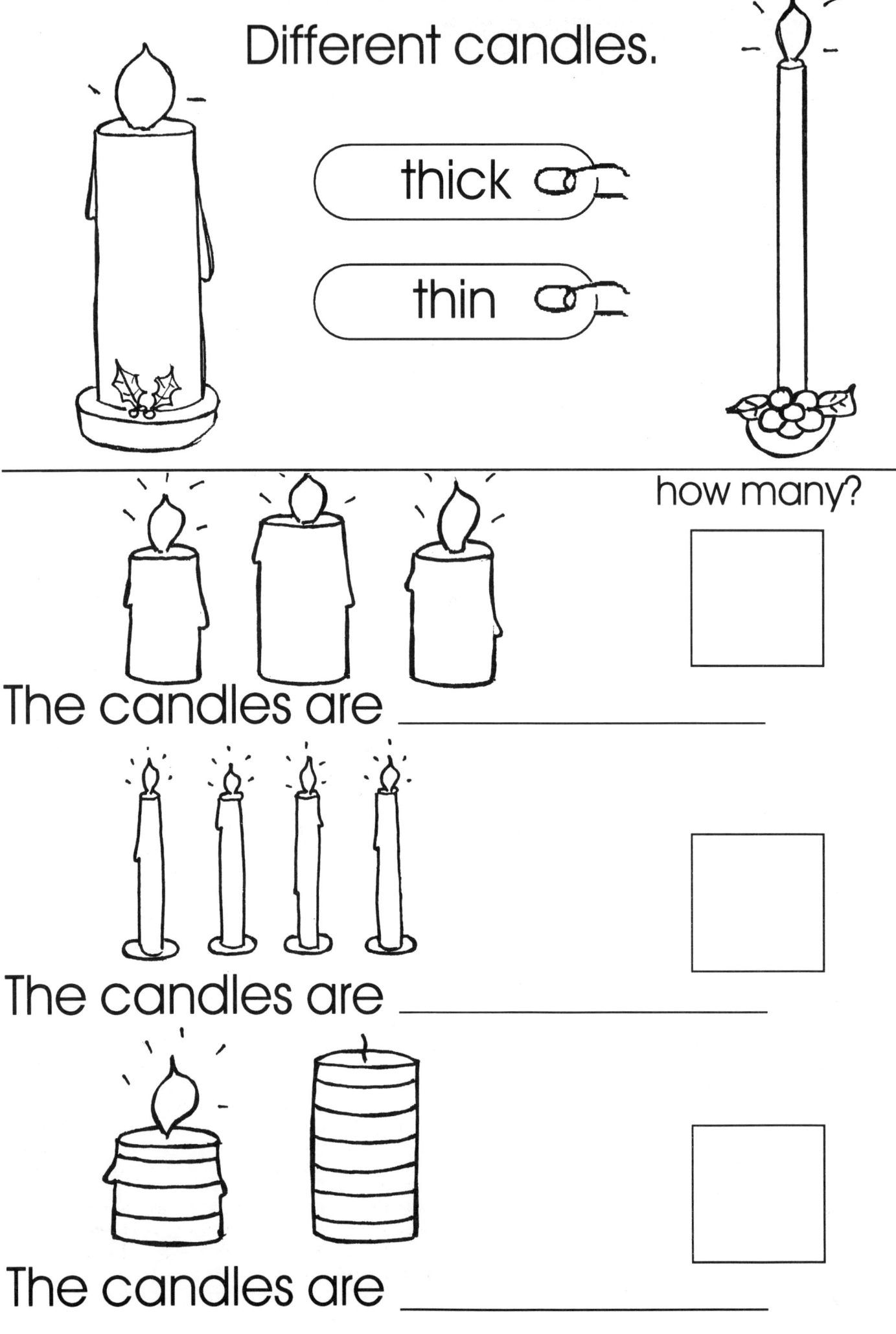

thick ⌐

thin ⌐

how many?

The candles are _____

The candles are _____

The candles are _____

Winter

All Kinds Of Winter Weather
• Look out of the window. Describe the weather today. What does the sky look like? Think of different kinds of winter weather - rain, hail, frost, snow, fog, strong winds and gales, sleet - and discuss.
• Children colour and cut around the pictures and put into sets - 'weather I like/don't like. Or stick onto paper with a sentence, eg. 'I like the snow because I can build a snowman.' etc.
• Children design own weather symbols and keep a winter weather chart, recording weather conditions for a whole month. Compare weather on first/last day of month. Have we had more rainy/fine days?

Jack Frost
• Go outside on a frosty day. Look at patterns on leaves, windows, frost on spider's webs. What does frost look like, feel like? What colour is it? Find out what happens when you breath on it.
• Discuss 'cold colours' (blue, silver, white). Have available crayons in various shades of blue and, white/silver glitter. Children complete Jack Frost by joining the dots and colouring in blue. Sprinkle with white/silver glitter to make him look frosty. Cut out labels and stick onto correct body parts.
• Sing 'Look out, look out' Carey Bonner, 'Child Songs'. 'Ho, Jack Frost', 'Harlequin'. A&C Black.

Match The Snowman
• Read 'Snow', Ian McMillan & Martyn Wiley, 'My red poetry book'. McMillan. Discuss all the fun things that we can do in the snow - throw snowballs, build snowmen, sledge, ski, etc. Think about the difficulties that snow brings, especially to the old folk. Draw a picture/write sentences.
• Children draw lines to match the snowmen and colour to match.
• Look at pictures of snowflakes - how they always make a six-pointed star. Make a snowflake pattern by folding a circle into six and cutting pieces from it.
What makes snow melt? Fill a jar with snow and let it melt in the classroom. How much water comes from it?

Build A Snowman
• Sing 'I'm a little snowman' Devon county play groups assoc. Foxlair. Talk to the children about what is needed to build a snowman and how they would do it. What could be used for eyes, nose, mouth? Make a recipe for a snowman.
• Make a 'snow scene' on a large piece of grey paper children draw a line 2/3 from top. Colour/cut out the snowman pieces and assemble on paper. Cover the bottom of the paper in cotton wool and add small cotton wool flakes in the sky. Sprinkle with glitter.
• Read and watch the video 'The Snowman' Raymond Briggs.

In The Snow
• Take the children for a winter's walk on a snowy day. Choose two children to walk on unspoilt snow. How do we know which way they went? Are their tracks the same? How do we know who made which footprints? Investigate shoe patterns/sizes. Look for animal tracks - cats, dogs, birds, horse. Did you find any vehicle tracks?
• Children discuss the tracks on the sheet, match and label.
• Use some old boots/shoes and make footprints by painting the soles and pressing onto paper.

How Do We Keep Warm
• Ask the caretaker to show you the school boiler and explain how it works. Follow the pipes around the school/count the radiators. How can we prevent 'cold' coming into the school? Design posters to remind people not to waste energy/keep the doors closed.
• Discuss ways of keeping ourselves/homes warm. Colour/cut out the pictures. Stick onto paper with sentences eg. 'Hot food and drinks help to keep us warm', 'I snuggle up in bed with a hot water bottle' etc.
• Make block graphs of 'Our favourite hot drinks', 'How we heat our homes', 'Colour of our winter coats' etc.
Invite gran/grandad to talk about how they kept warm in winter when they were young. What are the differences between now and then?

Warm Clothes
• Choose a child to put on his outdoor clothes - trousers, coat, scarf, hat, boots, mittens/gloves. Talk about the material from which they are made and how they keep us warm. Have fun sticking labels onto the child's clothes.
• Display the clothes on a table. Children complete the sheet by labelling the clothes, using those on the table as reference. Follow instructions for colouring.
• Collect four plastic bottles and make cardboard faces. Wrap in quilted fabric, aluminium foil, cotton, woollen fabric. Fill with hot water and place on window sill. After a period of time, test again to see which is the warmest/coolest. What does this tell us about the different materials? Record results.

Warm Hands And Feet
• Have available pairs of slippers, boots, gloves, mittens for the children to sort into pairs. Discuss how they help to keep us warm (made from wool/waterproof materials), with fleecy/furry linings etc. Why do we need to keep our feet and hands warm?
• Children use the sheet by identifying the pairs and colouring to match. Draw two large circles on a piece of paper, cut out 'hands' and 'feet' labels and stick one above each circle. Cut around the 'pairs' and put into the correct circle.
• Children draw around hands, colour as a pair of gloves and cut out. Glue at random onto a display board and match the gloves with string. Read 'Cold'. Shirley Hughes. 'Out and about'. Walker books.

Feeding The Birds In Winter

•Sing 'Little birds in winter time', 'Someone's singing Lord.' A&C Black. Set up a bird table outside the classroom window. Encourage the children bring suitable food to put on the table - bread, seeds, nuts, fat, fruit etc. Hang a nut bag from the table and watch the birds hang onto it. Try and identify some of the birds. Ask the question 'Why do we need to feed the birds in winter time?'

•Discuss the sheet with the children. Talk about position - above, on, under. Ask the children where the birds are in relation to the bird table. Count/number/colour the birds. draw three more birds under the table.

•Read 'Marcus Able and the birds' p79 'Tinderbox' Assembly book. Make a 'bird cake'. Make a knot in the end of a piece of string and thread through a hole in the bottom of a yoghurt pot. Put bread crumbs, peanuts, chopped bacon rind etc. into a bowl. Melt 4oz lard in a saucepan (a job for an adult) and pour into the bowl. Mix well and put into the yoghurt pot with a spoon. Press and wait until it 'sets'. Hang from the bird table.

Looking At Holly

•Take some sprigs of holly with berries into the classroom. Talk about the colours. Children examine the leaves. Look for opposites - shiny/dull, smooth/prickly. Explain that holly is an 'evergreen'. What other trees/bushes do you know that keep their leaves in winter? Look at books and pictures, make lists, draw pictures, bring in samples of leaves etc., and compare.

•Children count the leaves on one side of the sheet, and berries on the other, match to a number and colour.

•Take the children outside to look at the outlines of deciduous trees. Look at the way the branches are arranged. Measure the trunks of the trees with pieces of string. Examine twigs from the trees, make bark rubbings etc.

The School Nativity Play

•Tell the story of the Nativity to the children. Visit a local church to look at the Christmas crib. Have available a Christmas crib with a Nativity scene , and label.

•Discuss the figures in 'the school play' on the sheet and colour. Children use the Nativity scene as a reference and label their picture. Add a 'donkey' and 'a star'.

•With the children, plan and act out a Nativity play. Let the children 'write' the script, help with the costumes and help to make the props (crowns for the Kings, gifts).

Here Comes Santa Claus

•Sing 'When Santa got stuck down the chimney'. Have available picture of Santa Claus, cards, advent calenders etc. Talk about his appearance. Encourage adjectives to describe him - jolly, kind, fat. Make a large collage picture of Santa Claus, using paint, cotton wool, etc. With the children label 'beard', 'belt', 'boots', 'buttons'.

•Use the sheet as a phonic activity with letter 'b'. What can we see on Santa Claus that begins with 'b'. Children draw buttons and belt on his coat. Use the large collage as reference, cut out and stick on labels.

•Children paint a small cardboard box/carton to look like a chimney. Cut out the Santa and place him inside.

New Year

•Ask the children about how they celebrate New Year. 'Do you make special preparations, have special customs etc.?' 'Why do you think it is an important time to celebrate?' Make up 'New Year's resolutions', sing 'New things to do'. 'Tinderbox'. A&C Black.

•To make the calendar, children join the dots to finish the cat's face, colour all the body parts, and cut out carefully. Glue the ears onto the head by matching the small lines. Join other body parts together with paper fastener, matching the small circles. Stick a commercially produced calendar tab in the middle of the cat's body and attach a piece of brightly coloured ribbon in a loop to the back of the cat's head for hanging the calendar.

•Examine New Year's customs in other parts of the world eg. Chinese New Year, which falls between 20th January - 20th February. Learn the months of the year.

Shrove Tuesday

•Sing 'Shrove Tuesday' or 'Mix a pancake' Harlequin . A&C Black. Explain to the children that Shrove Tuesday is the day before Lent, which is a time of fasting and quietness. Shrove Tuesday used to be a day of mischief and fun when people ate up fancy foods, and also went to church to have their sins forgiven. Talk about various customs and games that take place, and foods that are eaten in towns and villages around the country.

•Children complete the tracking exercise and complete the sentence.

•Make pancakes. Sieve 250g plain flour into a large bowl, add 2 eggs, a pinch of salt, and mix. Slowly add 3/4 pint of milk, whisking continuously and making sure that there are no lumps. Watch an adult melt 25g of butter in the pan and add enough mixture to cover the bottom of the pan. When it is cooked, see if they can toss the pancake and catch it in the pan. Sprinkle sugar and lemon juice on the pancakes before eating.

All kinds of winter weather.

| rain | fog | ice | snow | frost | storm |

51

Jack Frost.

| fingers | toes | arm | leg | nose |

Match the snowmen.

Build a snowman.

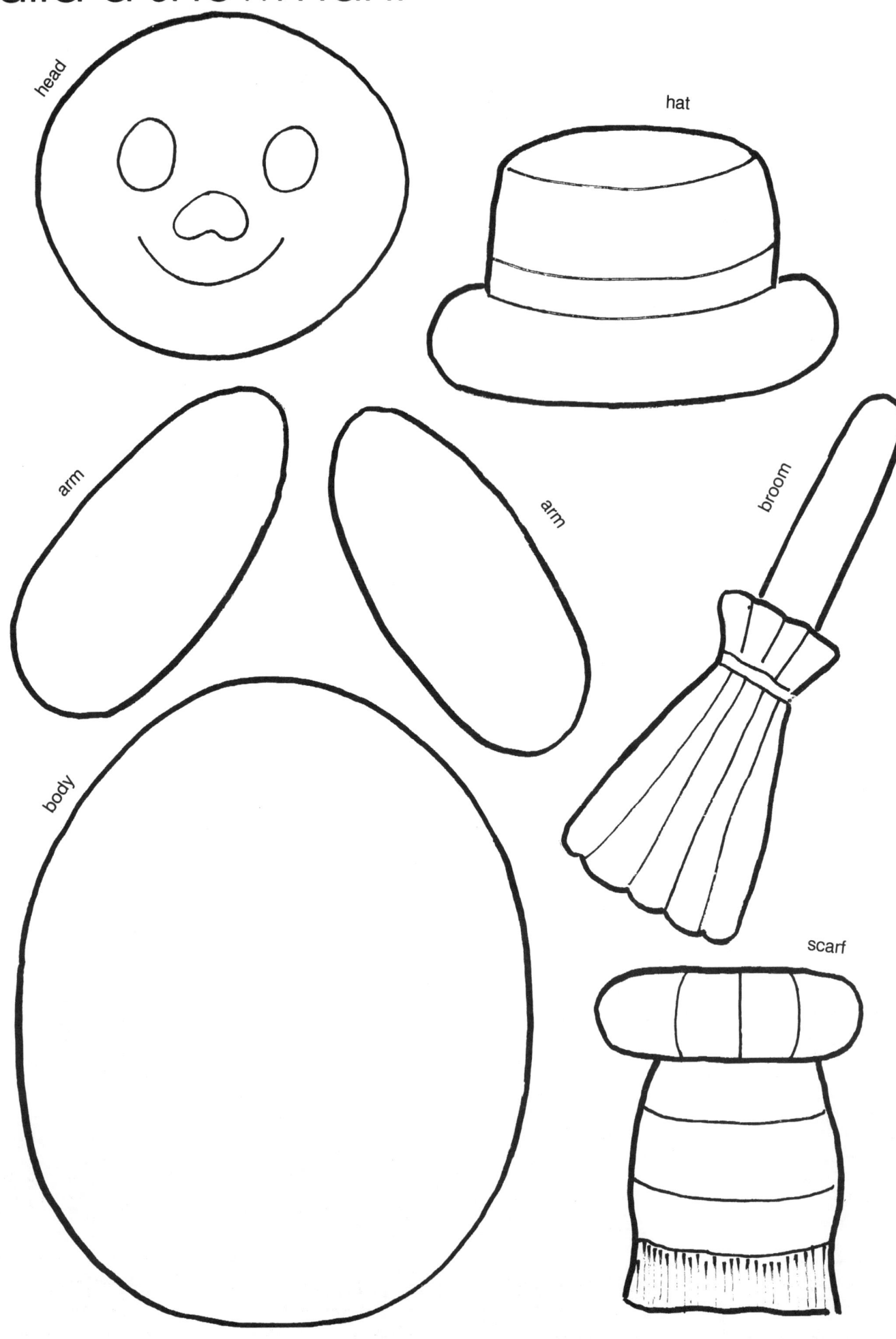

head

hat

arm

arm

broom

body

scarf

54

In the snow. Whose tracks?

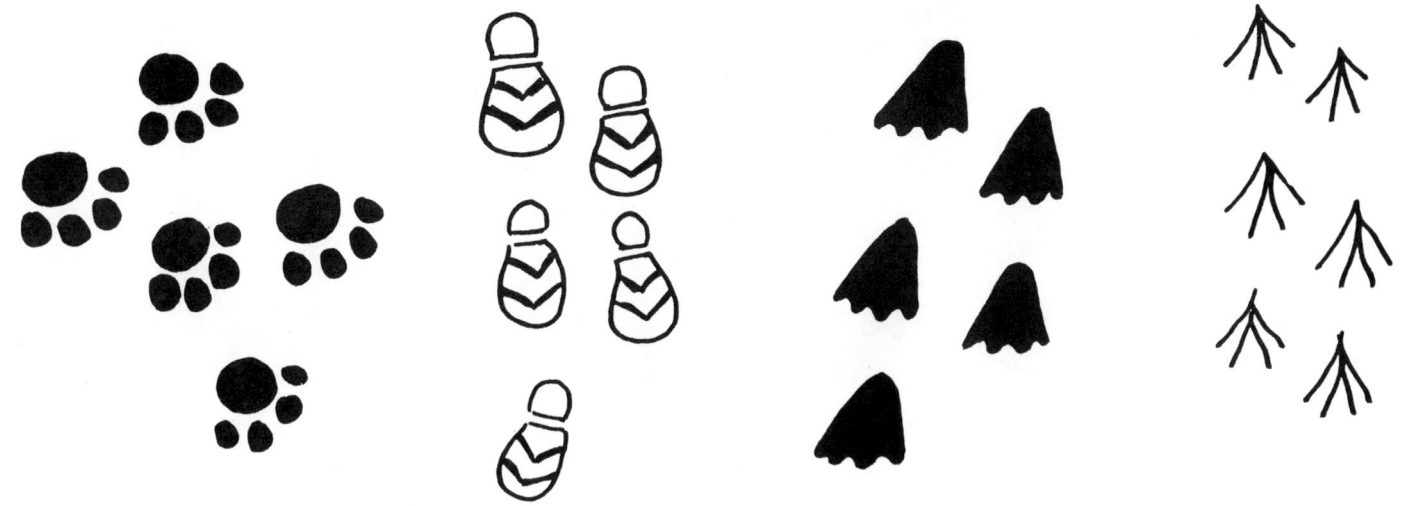

| hen | Sam | duck | cat |

How do we keep warm?

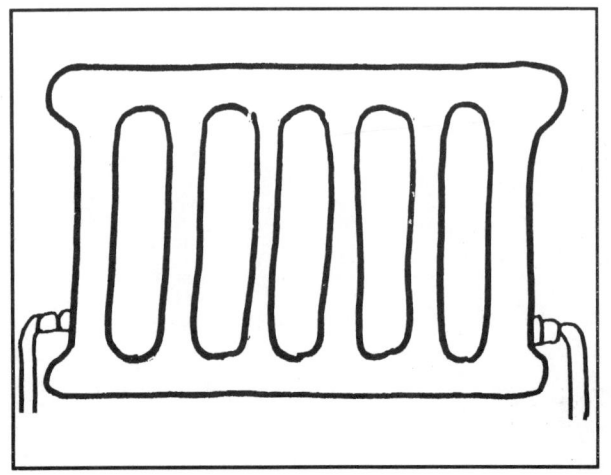

Warm clothes. Can you write the labels?

hat   mitten   boots   scarf   coat

Colour the coat red.
Colour the hat and scarf blue.

Warm hands and feet. Making Pairs.

 hands

 feet

Feeding the birds in winter.

☐ birds above the table.

☐ birds on the table.

☐ birds under the table

Draw 3 more birds under the table.

Looking at holly.

How many leaves?

How many berries?

The school Nativity play.

Joseph

three kings

Baby Jesus

an angel

Mary

shepherds

Here comes Santa Claus.

| boots | buttons | belt | beard |

New Year. A 'cat' calendar for you to make.

leg

tail

ear

Shrove Tuesday. The pancake race.
Who dropped the pancake?

Jack   Amy   Sam   Katy

_____ dropped the pancake.